T0375101

MULTIRACIAL PARENTS

Multiracial Parents

Mixed Families, Generational Change,
and the Future of Race

Miri Song

NEW YORK UNIVERSITY PRESS

New York

NEW YORK UNIVERSITY PRESS
New York
www.nyupress.org

References to Internet websites (URLs) were accurate at the time of writing. Neither the author nor New York University Press is responsible for URLs that may have expired or changed since the manuscript was prepared.

Library of Congress Cataloging-in-Publication Data
Names: Song, Miri, 1964– author.
Title: Multiracial parents : mixed families, generational change, and the future of race / Miri Song.
Description: New York : New York University, [2017] | Includes bibliographical references and index.
Identifiers: LCCN 2017003867 | ISBN 9781479840540 (cl : alk. paper) | ISBN 9781479825905 (pb : alk. paper)
Subjects: LCSH: Racially mixed families. | Parenting. | Race—Social aspects.
Classification: LCC HQ1031 .S66 2017 | DDC 306.85/05—dc23
LC record available at https://lccn.loc.gov/2017003867

New York University Press books are printed on acid-free paper, and their binding materials are chosen for strength and durability. We strive to use environmentally responsible suppliers and materials to the greatest extent possible in publishing our books.

Manufactured in the United States of America

10 9 8 7 6 5 4 3 2 1

Also available as an ebook

For Charlie Alexander Song-Smith and

Theo Myung-Do Song-Smith

CONTENTS

CONTENTS

ACKNOWLEDGMENTS

Of the books I have written thus far, I have most enjoyed writing this one. Having followed the work of many scholars of race and of multiracial people, I was very excited when I realized that there were no books that focused specifically on multiracial people who were parents. After working on the topic of "mixed-race" people for some years now, I had begun to feel that I had exhausted my interest in this area. But of course, I was wrong, as I became increasingly interested in generational change, and how "multigeneration" multiracial people would think about their ethnic and racial ancestries. Such questions are before me in my daily life, as I have watched my sons, Charlie and Theo, grow up.

I would like to thank the generosity of the Leverhulme Trust, which funded this research and enabled me to buy myself out of much of my teaching for several years. Like others who do qualitative research, I simply would not have been able to proceed without such a grant. In the course of my research, I was able to hear the stories of an amazing array of participants, who illustrated perfectly just how heterogeneous the rubric "multiracial" is. To these participants, who generously shared their time, feelings, and stories with me, I am extremely grateful. I would also like to thank the schools that granted me access to their parents. Thanks go to my research associate for the Leverhulme project, Caitlin Gutierrez O'Neill, who carried out some of the interviews, and who was integral to the analysis of the interview data. Working with Ilene Kalish at New York University Press has been a pleasure, and I thank her for her interest and professionalism.

A number of scholars in the United States showed interest, enthusiasm, and support for this research. Thanks to Jenifer Bratter, whose article actually inspired the idea for my broader, qualitative study in the first place, and to Wendy Roth, Ann Morning, and Vilna Treitler. Paul Spickard has, over the years, provided encouragement and mentoring, for which I'm very grateful. On this side of the pond, a number of people have provided not only wisdom, but interest in this project: Ros Edwards, Martin Bulmer, Caroline Knowles, Ravinder Barn, Chamion Caballero, Peter Aspinall, Ben Bowling, Elaine Bauer, and Brett St. Louis. John Solomos deserves special thanks for always being a quietly encouraging presence. As always, Les Back has been a friend who can invariably raise a smile and offer inspiration. In addition to engaging in discussions about our work, Becky King-O'Riain has been a reliable source of good food, wine, and fun. And on the increasingly distant continent, post-Brexit, Maurice Crul, Frans Lelie, Patrick Simon, Jens Schneider, and Dan Rodriguez-Garcia have been great colleagues and friends.

Parts of this book were written while I was the Willy Brandt Guest Professor at the University of Malmo Institute for the Studies of Migration, Diversity, and Welfare (MIM) between September 2013 and January 2014. Pieter Bevelander in particular was extremely generous with his time, energy, and interest, and it was wonderful to immerse myself in this institute. I would like to thank Erica Righard, Nahikari Irastorza, Sayaka Osanami Torngren, Christian Fernandez, Ingrid Ramsoy, Henrik Emilsson, Bjorn Frylund, Louise Tregert, and Merja Skaffali-Multala for making me feel so welcome. During that time in Malmo, I became a cyclist again, and learned also to appreciate the easy availability of wine and spirits in England! I also thank Russell King, who preceded me in Malmo, and who has been a supportive colleague over the years.

My then head of school (at the University of Kent), Sarah Vickerstaff, enabled me to take up this wonderful opportunity in Malmo and provided encouragement along the way. At the University of Kent, I have been fortunate to have a number of colleagues in the School of Social Policy, Sociology, and Social Research whose support and friendship made the writing of this book much more enjoyable than it could have been.

What would the process of writing be without friends who take an interest and who transport us away with fun, food, and drink? Over the years, my friends in Canterbury and farther afield have kept me entertained: Miguel Alexiades, Anna Chan, Abi Cooper, Eric Edgar, Cecily Fahey, Frank Garcia, David Herd, Pamela Kea, David Lewis, Diana Milanovic, Liza Miller, Daniela Peluso, Guy Roberts-Holmes, and Laurence Skillern. Many old friends in the US have also kept me afloat over the years, especially Jean-Christophe Castelli, Julia Dillon, Michael Hirschorn, Hillary Kruger, Susan Morris, and Sung-Hee Suh.

In addition to being "always there" for me and enabling me to pursue my interests (and the many jaunts abroad), Murray Smith has been a great partner and friend, and laundry czar with no equal. Charlie and Theo—thank you for showing interest in my work and for being the delightful and maddening creatures that you are. My sister, Vivian Song, and my brothers, Paul Song and Joe Song, and my parents, Moon-Won Song and Yung-Hee Park, continue to be hugely important, though you are all very far away. Vivian, in particular, has been incredibly important in my life—she has provided much mirth during the entire life of this project.

Introduction

Mixed People and "Mixing" in Today's Britain

My guess is, yes, it will dilute further and in the fullness of time, you know, me, my dad/mum, you know, that'll just become a little bit of family history and gradually that will, you know, sort of come down to a little dot somewhere and if somebody is really interested sort of look back a hundred years they'll say, "Oh yes, there was a sort of Indian in our family at some point."
—Drew (South Asian/White, 47)

Drew, who had an Indian father and English mother and who grew up in mostly White towns in England, reflected upon whether and how his Indian ancestry will be transmitted down the generations. As a mixed-race person, with a White British partner and children who looked entirely White, he believed such "dilution" to be just a matter of time. Since there is no one typical narrative about the meanings and significance of minority ancestries for the multiracial individuals in this study, this book explores the various ways in which they have thought about their status and experiences as mixed people, as well as how they have identified and raised their children. An investigation into the experiences of multiracial people and their families is highly topical, as mixed people and unions are increasingly common in many parts of Britain—as well as other highly diverse societies such as that of the United States. As a recent article put it,

> Mixed-race relationships are now so common that some ethnic groups— starting with African Caribbean—will virtually disappear, the research states. Young people are six times more likely to be mixed-race as adults.

Experts believe the findings, which come just days after Prince Harry was rebuked for calling a fellow cadet "Paki," and Prince Charles admitted to referring to an Asian friend as "Sooty," mean that future generations "will not see race in the way we see it."[1]

This excerpt from the *Observer*, which refers to a study commissioned by the Equality and Human Rights Commission (EHRC), is striking in a number of respects. But one particular assertion is especially notable: it is that specific ethnic groups, such as African Caribbean, may "disappear."

Given the historical denigration of African origin people in many societies around the world and the continuing racial tensions which surround Black-White relations in the United States in particular, such a notion may be difficult to imagine, but in Britain, the very significant growth in interracial unions is destabilizing traditional understandings of ethnic and racial categories, which are premised upon the popular and longstanding belief that people can be straightforwardly assigned to monoracial (that is, single-race) categories, such as Black, Asian, or White. At the same time, as the above quotation suggests, the blurring and possible demise of ethnic categories (such as African Caribbean) sits alongside the still not uncommon usage of offensive racial shibboleths and stereotypes.

Despite (or because of) the growing commonality of mixed people and unions, societal concerns about the "place" of multiracial people and ambivalence about ethnic and racial "mixing" in Britain persist. When a short film (by the film director Danny Boyle) created for the opening ceremony of the 2012 summer Olympics held in London depicted the typical British family as a mixed one—one with a White mother, a Black father, and two mixed daughters—one conservative media outlet, the *Daily Mail*, which is one of the most popular tabloid newspaper in Britain, famously scorned this representation of Britain, calling such a depiction of a mixed family "absurdly unrealistic" and "politically correct": "This was supposed to be a representation of modern life in England but it is likely to be a challenge for the organisers to find an educated white middle-aged mother and black father living together with a happy family in such a set-up."[2] In response to a storm of criticism, the *Daily Mail* removed this piece from its website. And the fact is, such a depiction of family life resonates for many families in London and other British cities and towns.

Analysts have argued that a polarized discourse has emerged in Britain, in which "images of racial, ethnic and faith diversity are posed in opposition to societal unity and solidarity, with assertions that these differences create a crisis of cohesive national social trust" (as is suggested in the *Daily Mail* piece above).[3] Rosalind Edwards and her colleagues argue that "sweeping portrayals of segregation and conflict ignore the reality of ongoing local interactions between a mix of minority and majority racial, ethnic and religious cultures, where multi-culture is ordinary."[4] So if forms of mixing are increasingly ordinary, how important are ethnic and racial backgrounds to multiracial people and their families?

Turning to the considerable scholarship on multiracial people in the United States, a recent national survey of 1,555 multiracial Americans aged 18 and older (of various "mixes") by the Pew Research Center found that "for multiracial adults, as for the general public, race is not the most important element of their personal identity. Some 26% of multiracial adults say their racial background is 'essential' to their identity (as do 28% of all adults)."[5] In fact, this study found that both multiracial adults and the general public are much more likely to identify gender and religion as central to their sense of selves. In other words, we cannot presume the automatic salience of "race" in the lives of American multiracial people—or, as other studies have found, in those of multiracial young people in Britain.[6]

This book explores these different currents of social continuity and change in contemporary British society through a study of multiracial (or "mixed-race"/"mixed") people and their children. In doing so, it takes the study of multiracial people down a generation.

As Britain and many other multiethnic societies become ever more diverse, societal awareness of and discourses about ethnic and racial difference (and the taxonomies that accompany such discourses, both official and colloquial) become more pervasive, whether in the media or in numerous instances of "real life." Beliefs about the embodiment of race and racial difference are still with us, even though there is now relatively widespread awareness, especially in educated middle-class circles, of the socially constructed nature of race. In fact, there is ample evidence that many people in the wider society still subscribe to the fixity and seemingly enduring nature of race and racial differences.

For instance, In October 2013, a seven-year-old girl with blonde hair and blue eyes was removed from her home in Dublin, despite her Roma parents' insistence that they were her parents. After a DNA test proved that she was indeed this couple's child, the Irish police and health services were forced into an embarrassing U-turn.[7] The removal of this child, along with that of a two-year-old boy from another Roma family, was justified by concerns that these children did not resemble their darker Roma parents or siblings. In another recent case, in the United States, a White woman named Jennifer Cramblett became pregnant through artificial insemination, but the sperm bank mistakenly provided sperm from a Black donor, instead of from the White donor whom she and her partner had selected.[8] As a result, Cramblett was shocked to give birth to a mixed-race daughter. Cramblett professes to loving her daughter, but argued that she was wholly unprepared to raise a part Black, mixed-race child, as she had "limited cultural competency" with African Americans.[9] Such thinking, based upon established conventions regarding the importance of parents not only resembling their offspring, but also demonstrating ethnic and racial awareness in the raising of ethnic minority children, is still widespread. Questions about the significance (or not) of ethnic and racial backgrounds imbue various contemporary policy debates, such as those concerning transracial adoption. Passed under a Conservative government, the Children and Families Act of 2014 essentially removes the previous requirement for issues of "ethnicity" (race, religion, language and culture) to be taken into account in adoption decisions.[10]

Nonetheless, it remains the case that families with members who are deemed to be not of the same "race," phenotypically, are suspect. The presence of a blonde child within a Roma family setting immediately evokes a sense of disorder, of things out of place, as famously theorized by the anthropologist Mary Douglas.[11] Among the myriad issues and concerns that can arise for parents of *any* children, it is undeniable that in many public settings, parents and children who are regarded as being visibly of different "races" can often engender stares, suspicion (as the cases above illustrate), and sometimes even hostility.

While there are also studies showing that some people subscribe to notions of dormant racial traits, which can unexpectedly appear in later generations (as "throwbacks") to explain physical incongruities between parents and their children,[12] such views do not disrupt the normative *expectation* that parents and children should resemble each other racially. In fact, such notions of "throwback" can be spoken of with trepidation, revealing the fears many still have of "miscegenation." Despite the fact that decades of research have pointed to the complex intertwining of genetic and environmental factors in explaining many social outcomes, some analysts have warned that there has been a worrying resurgence in attention given to the biological status of race and racial inheritance in mainstream social science.[13]

Furthermore, so entrenched are our notions of racial difference and our tendency to differentiate people in relation to racial taxonomies, that when individuals violate these "natural" categories and claim membership in a group to which they were not born, in terms of ethnic and racial parentage, they can cause uproar. While the policing of such racial chicanery has historically been in relation to fears about non-White people "passing" as White, in June 2015, the case of Rachel Dolezal, a White woman in the United States who presented herself as a Black person with Black ancestry, engendered an outpouring of anger and outrage by many commentators. Dolezal was "outed" by her parents, who revealed that she had wholly White ancestry. The ensuing controversy resulted in widespread debates about whether race is primarily a physical and immutable birthright or something that can be cultural and adopted.[14] Dolezal's case also sparked fascinating discussions about whether her claim to feel African American was analogous to Caitlyn Jenner's claim that she was really a woman trapped in a man's body.[15]

Who Comprises the Multiracial Population?

The growth of mixed people and families makes such debates about our understandings of ethnic and racial difference, as well as of ethnic options, even more pressing, since multiracial people, by definition, transcend monoracial categorization.[16] Increasingly, multiracial people are identifying in a variety of ways, and the formal recognition of multiracial people (since 2001) is illustrated by the England and Wales decennial census in which "Mixed"[17] is an option in response to the question: "What is your ethnic group"? How people answer this question is a matter of choice,[18] and how parents identify themselves and their children on official forms (and in everyday life) may not always correspond with their (or their children's) actual ethnic or racial parentage.[19]

Interestingly, while there is no one official definition of "Mixed" in Britain, the Office for National Statistics does provide a definition of "interethnic" marriages as being between people from different *aggregate ethnic groups*, where the ethnic group categories are: White, Mixed, Asian [meaning South Asian], Black, Chinese, Other ethnic group.[20] Thus, one can deduce that the term "Mixed" is meant to refer to individuals comprising specific combinations that (usually) include White and one of the broad "aggregate ethnic groups" such as "Black" or "Asian."[21] But a more recent ONS paper on "inter-ethnic unions" (drawing on the 2011 census) conceptualizes such unions quite differently,[22] suggesting the changeable and contested ways in which official bodies conceive of "mixing" or mixture.

In this book, I use the terms "multiracial," "mixed race," and "mixed" interchangeably to refer to individuals who have parents who are considered to be of disparate racial ancestries (in keeping with beliefs about the essential nature of "race" and racial differences), and who are visibly different from each other according to dominant social norms (such as Black/White, or East Asian/White). In the British context, "Black" can refer to people of Black Caribbean or Black African origin, "South Asian" refers to people with ancestry from the Indian subcontinent, while "East Asian" refers to people with ancestry from either East or Southeast Asia.

The growing attention to "mixture" and "mixing" is also reflected in burgeoning studies about multiracial children and people in Britain, most typically focusing upon how such individuals racially identify. However, no studies in Britain (or in the United States) have looked specifically at *multiracial people as parents* and their relationships with their own children—that is, there has been no study of how multiracial people think about the next generation down, their second-generation mixed children. And as these second-generation mixed individuals grow up, partner, and have children themselves, we are facing a fascinating yet unknown societal landscape.

This book thus breaks new ground by taking the now sizeable body of literature on multiracial people one step further—another generation down—given that many multiracial people in Britain and the United States are no longer children or young people, but are now parents. As most official classification systems and policies (equal opportunity or anti-discrimination, for example) are premised upon monoracial categories, the existence of multiracial people and their children poses serious questions about the validity of such frameworks. Demographically and socially, we must face the reality of multigeneration multiracial people and families, and this book is one of the first to explore this increasingly common phenomenon.

In the context of the rapid growth of interracial unions and mixed people, individuals may not always know very much about their minority ancestries or the specific locus of "mixture" in generational terms. Related to this, there is considerable societal interest in finding out about one's ancestral roots, as evidenced by the proliferation of websites and software to populate one's family tree, as well as television series such as the BBC's *Who Do You Think You Are?* or the US series *Finding Your Roots* hosted by Henry Louis Gates. In the case of African Americans (and some Britons of Caribbean backgrounds), whose ancestors were enslaved in the trans-Atlantic passage, reclaiming a lost African heritage can be of tremendous emotional and political significance. Alondra Nelson found that African Americans have engaged in genetic DNA testing to locate the African region from where their slave ancestors originated.[23] These various ways in which people seek to excavate their ancestral pasts may also be indicative of a need for what Anthony Giddens refers to as "ontological security"[24] in light of the often fast-paced and changeable worlds we inhabit. And despite the increasingly diverse types of family and routes to parenthood,[25] societal discourses and norms about the legitimacy and racial "purity" of ancestral descent can bear especially on multiracial people and their families.

A Look across the Atlantic

As an American who grew up in the United States, but who has lived in England since 1991, I find that many American studies view race relations and the significance of race and racisms (not surprisingly) through an American lens, without necessarily recognizing that an American framework does not apply universally. In fact, some scholars do not seem to want to hear about how people in different societies may think differently about race. The research (upon which this book is based) grew out of my interest and engagement with quantitative studies in the United States, some of which assumed that parents' racial categorizations of their multiracial children told the whole story—that their "tick boxes" told us all we needed to know about how interracial couples thought about ethnic and racial identification and how they were raising their children. I find these assumptions to be problematic. Given the high rate of interracial partnering in Britain, Britain provides a wonderful comparative test case.

Studies of race and ethnic minority groups find it difficult to situate multiracial people in a racially stratified society, which is usually understood in relation to the hierarchical positionings of monoracial groups. The question of how to assess the *children of multiracial people*, that is, second-generation multiracials, who are often several generations removed from a minority ancestor(s), requires even more debate and investigation. As I argue in this book, no clear conventions apply in this context. Is there a generational "tipping point" at which one's minority ancestry ceases to be meaningful for multiracial individuals and their children—especially for multiracial people with predominantly White ancestors? Can such tipping points be reversed by new patterns of mixing, ones that don't always involve White people and/or forms of ethnic and racial revivals?

The status and experiences of multiracial people need to be investigated, but given the heterogeneity of such a population, what we know is still largely speculative. Thus, this book considers these key questions:

1. How do *multiracial people* (as opposed to those in interracial unions) racially identify their children, and on what bases do multiracial people make such choices?
2. How do multiracial people raise their children? Is there a clear correspondence between how they racially identify their children and how they raise them?
3. Is a mixed-race identity, or a specific minority heritage, something that mixed-race parents wish to transmit to their children?
4. How may the specific "race mixture" and racial experiences of the mixed-race parent and the racial background(s) of his or her spouse influence the identification and socialization of his or her children?
5. Do multiracial people think that their children are or will be subject to forms of racial prejudice and discrimination?

6. What is in store for multiracial people and their children? Is there a generational tipping point at which one's mixedness and/or minority ancestry becomes inconsequential?

Why is this study of multiracial people and their children of social importance? These multiracial individuals are raising the next generation, and as such, they provide a valuable glimpse into how ethnic and racial identification and difference may or may not matter as their children become adults. It is also important to investigate the approaches and practices adopted by these parents, as their experiences of parenthood are likely to differ considerably from those of multiracial people of an earlier generation (such as their parents), when mixed relationships and families were both less common and less socially acceptable.

The Study

Investigating the views, experiences, and practices of multiracial people as parents is clearly no small task and required gathering a great deal of data about not only each participant's life history, but also that of his or her family. Complementing and extending existing studies employing census data, a qualitative approach allows us to ask a different set of questions about the "hows" and "whys" of various processes. An in-depth qualitative investigation also allows us to open up and disaggregate "the family"—not just down the generations, but also in such a way as to enable participants to reflect on their experiences, choices, and practices in comparison to those of their parents, as well as the experiences of their children. Not only are multiracial people in Britain extremely heterogeneous, but, as discussed throughout this book, it is clear that we cannot extrapolate much reliable information on the basis of census categories specifying ethnic and racial identification. How multiracial people of various backgrounds think about their mixed ancestries, live their lives, and raise their children cannot be properly understood without attending to their detailed life histories and accounts of themselves.

The Participants

Of the 62 multiracial participants in this study, 37 were women and 25 men, and most were aged between 25 and 50, though a small number of participants were in their fifties, and the eldest was 62. The age of children in these households varied from a few months old to late twenties. Depending on the age of our participants, most of the parents either had children of primary school age and/or younger or had children in both primary and secondary schools. Of the 62 participants, all of whom had had children in heterosexual unions, 14 were not partnered at the time of the study, with most of these being separated or divorced from their former partners.

The study participants had to meet the following criteria. First, each one had to be a parent. Second, all participants had to have one White and one non-White parent, such as an East Asian mother and a White father. Most commonly, the White parents were White British, but this sample also included those with a White parent of other European backgrounds, such as French. Participants could also have one White parent and one multiracial parent. Either way, given the debates about whether some multiracial people would wish to claim a White identity for their children, if given the opportunity to do so, it was important that one parent be White. Rather than choosing participants who identified as mixed, only individuals who reported minority (or multiracial) and White *ancestries* (regardless of how they identified themselves) were included in this study.

While there are no established conventions in Britain for who can be said to be multiracial, per se, the mixed backgrounds of the individuals in this study—32 Black/White, 19 South Asian/White, 11 East Asian/White—reflect the most common mixed ancestries in Britain.[26] In the online surveys, participants were more or less detailed in how they reported their ethnic and racial ancestries, so that while some may have specified that they were "Black Jamaican and English," others used the shorthand of "Black/White." For the purposes of facilitating comparisons, I distilled the open-ended responses about mixed ancestries into the three broad types of mixed ancestries above.

Had time and resources been unlimited, I would have liked to include mixed participants who were "minority mix" and who had no (known) White parentage. However, in addition to the fact that such mixed people are still relatively few in Britain, I wanted to focus upon how multiracial status and experience were affected by generational change, especially for those who had a White parent. I specifically excluded participants who were the children of *interethnic* unions (such as between a White British and White German), as I wanted participants who had grown up with parents who were regarded as being of two visibly distinct "races," according to prevailing social norms.

While most (54 of 62) participants were first-generation mixed, with one White and one non-White minority parent, 7 participants were second-generation mixed, meaning they had at least one parent who was multiracial. Moreover, one participant was not entirely sure about whether one of her parents was mixed or not (I counted only those who were certain that one of their parents was mixed as second-generation mixed). The majority of participants (46 of 62) had White British (38) or White other (8 non-British) partners with whom they had children. By comparison, 9 participants had partners with a monoracial minority background (3 British and 6 non-British), and 7 had multiracial partners (4 British and 3 non-British). Those partners who had grown up in another country and not attended school in Britain were categorized as ethnically non-British. A small number of participants had had children with more than one partner; in those cases, I recorded only the backgrounds of the first partner with whom they had had children.

Several important limitations arose from the small sample in this study. Had I been able to obtain a larger and more representative sample, I could have explored the gender dimensions of multiracial experiences more fully, given that female participants with young children were usually the primary caregivers. In addition, there is evidence that racial identification among multiracial people is gendered, with women more likely than men to identify as multiracial.[27]

Furthermore, considering the potentially significant influence that class and affluence can have on how minority people racially identify themselves, the predominantly middle-class profile of the participants is likely to have provided only a partial picture of how mixed people thought about and experienced their roles as parents and their day-to-day lives more generally. The majority of participants were middle class, meaning that they had either a first degree in higher education and/or professional forms of employment (such as university lecturer or financial consultant). Of the 62 participants, 10 had not been university educated, and had relatively low-skilled and/or clerical forms of employment, such as a school "dinner lady" or call center worker. Those participants who were middle class also typically had one or more parents who were (or had been) themselves relatively highly educated and/or in professional occupations.

Lastly, there is little doubt that regional variation in how people think about and experience their multiracial backgrounds remains significant, and while I was able to distinguish between those in urban versus more suburban settings, most of the participants in this study were drawn from the South East of England. Most of the 62 participants resided in the Greater London area and cities and towns in the South East, but a small proportion lived in cities and towns in the Midlands and the North. In addition, we included 2 participants who lived in Wales and Scotland, respectively. Participants' residential locations and their children's schools varied considerably in terms of their ethnic and racial diversity. While participants living in London and other large cities tended to live in ethnically diverse areas (usually with relatively diverse schools), those residing in small towns and cities outside of London and other large metropolitan areas reported predominantly White neighborhoods and schools for their children.

Data Collection and Analysis

Not surprisingly, in a small, qualitative study of this kind, achieving a representative sample of multiracial people in Britain was not possible. Through schools, websites, and snowball sampling, we recruited 62 mixed-race parents, each of whom completed an online survey, followed by an in-depth interview. After we obtained permission from gate-keepers, such as head teachers, brief letters describing the nature and aims of the project were disseminated by schools directly—either via hard copy to all parents or via email attachments sent out by the school. Advertisements were also placed on some websites aimed at mixed individuals and families in Britain, such as Intermix (www.intermix.org.uk) and People in Harmony (www.pih.org.uk). Overall, 19 participants were recruited through schools, 22 through websites, and 21 through snow-balling. We did not discern any notable differences in the participants or data based upon the mode of recruitment—though those who were recruited via websites aimed at multiracial people and families could have had a greater awareness and investment in their status as mixed people.

There were two stages to data collection, which were carried out between July 2012 and December 2013. First, the online surveys elicited mostly factual background information about participants' histories, including their place of birth, where they attended primary and secondary schools, and the ethnic backgrounds of their parents, among many other variables. For instance, participants were asked to respond to the following question: "How would you describe your 'mixed' background? (Please be as specific as possible, and describe both your mother's and father's ancestries. If one or both of your parents is 'mixed' themselves, please specify their ancestries)." The online survey used open-response fields, so that participants could use their own terms and language to describe themselves and their families.

These surveys were followed by in-depth semi-structured interviews, which gathered detailed information about participants' family and individual histories, along with their thoughts and experiences as multiracial individuals and as parents. They were also probed about the descriptions of their mixed backgrounds in their online surveys. These interviews were crucial in providing a sense of the participants' day-to-day lives with their children and in their wider social networks. Most interviews were conducted in the participants' homes, though about one third were conducted in the participants' offices and/or public spaces such as cafes and restaurants. These interviews ranged from one and a half to three hours. While most of the participants were very forthcoming and open about discussing their life experiences and those of their children, in a handful of interviews, not all of the data collection was complete due to participants having limited time and needing to terminate the interviews before all the topics had been covered; in a few of those cases, we were unable to secure a follow-up interview to complete the data collection. All the interviews were recorded using a digital voice recorder, then transcribed verbatim (as soon as possible after the interviews took place). In a few cases, face-to-face interviews were not possible, and so they were conducted via Skype, and in one instance, telephone. Pseudonyms were used for all participants, and personal details were changed in some cases to ensure anonymity. While we had not initially planned on photographing the participants, early on in the research, we asked them permission to do so or to send us a photograph of their choice. With a few exceptions, the participants agreed, and their photographs were helpful in completing a portrayal of each participant.

While Statistical Package for the Social Sciences (SPSS) was used to identify some overall patterns found in the online survey, the analysis of the interview data was wholly qualitative. As researchers, we engaged in an interpretation of the interview transcripts.[28] A thematic analysis of the interviews started with jotting down notes about particular themes or points that had been especially prominent. Notes about the emotional tenor of the interviews were also recorded, as it was not uncommon for participants to articulate a range of often strong emotions, as they reflected upon their lives and those of their children. Observations were scribbled along the margins of transcripts, as well as when listening to the digital recordings themselves several times, and then we created codes to reflect key themes.[29] An effort was made to compare the thoughts and experiences of participants of different ethnic and racial ancestries, as well as a range of participants living in diverse urban areas and those living in largely White and more suburban locations. Our approach generally approximates what Anselm Strauss and Juliet Corbin refer to as "open coding," or "the process of breaking down, examining, comparing, conceptualizing, and categorizing data."[30] Accordingly, we generated a set of codes, with their definitions, to cover the full range of themes, practices, and ideas in the interview transcripts.

Overview of the Book

While many studies of multiracial people have been carried out in the United States in the last several decades, the study of multiracial people and their families is still relatively nascent in Britain. Chapter 1 begins with a discussion of the demographic growth of mixed people in Britain and shows that, rather than constituting a marginal social group, multiracial people in Britain are quickly becoming more numerous, especially in ethnically diverse metropolitan areas. After reviewing both North American and British studies, this chapter also demonstrates that there is a significant gap in the research concerning *mixed-race people as parents* and their relationships with their children. This generational perspective, I argue, is needed to achieve a fuller understanding of what it means to be a multiracial individual and parent today.

Chapter 2 examines how and why multiracial people identify their children in particular ways. Amazingly, we know very little about this key question. Do participants of disparate mixed backgrounds differ in the identifications of their children? Do the ethnic and racial backgrounds of partners influence how they identify their children? Furthermore, how important is the physical appearance of children, the generational locus of mixture, and contact with White and ethnic minority family members in shaping the identification of children? While many US studies have focused on how parents in interracial unions racially classify their children, these studies have not investigated how such parents think about or explain their choices. As I demonstrate in this chapter, the racial categories chosen by multiracial people—whether "mixed," "Black," "White," "Asian," or others—do not speak for themselves. Rather, they need to be unpacked, as the meanings and motivations underlying the use of such terms are far from straightforward.

In fact, the identification of children on official forms can tell us only so much about how multiracial people actually raise their children—the focus of Chapter 3. As some analysts have pointed out, monoracial parents in interracial relationships will not have experienced many of the issues and concerns that can arise for their children. Do multiracial people, as parents, steer their children in terms of cultural transmission and/or racial awareness in their upbringing? Is there a correspondence between how parents racially identify and how they raise their children? In this chapter, I examine several ways in which multiracial people bring up their children, and I examine why particular parents are drawn to specific modes of socialization. Furthermore, I discuss the importance of generational change and how participants' experiences of their own upbringings and childhoods can influence their thinking and parenting practices.

Chapter 4 then turns to a significant concern for many multiracial parents: Will their children be subject to forms of racial prejudice and discrimination? How do parents teach their children about the realities of race, and how do they prepare them to deal with potential forms of discrimination and denigration? While existing studies of mixed people in Britain rarely explicitly address their experiences of racial stigmatization or denigration, even less is known about how they, as parents, regard the racialized experiences of their children. In this chapter, I examine how multiracial participants' own experiences of racism (or lack thereof) may influence potential concerns about how their own children are treated in the wider society. The interviews with our participants reveal a strong theme of generational change and norms, which involves the need and obligation on the part of some parents to discuss racial awareness and coping—though how parents put this into practice can differ in their day-to-day lives.

Not surprisingly, our participants' accounts of themselves and their children often segued into both the past and the future. Chapter 5 thus addresses how our participants reflected upon what was in store for their children as they grew up and perhaps had children of their own. Here, I consider what multiracial parents thought about the salience of ethnic and racial difference in the future and what this would portend for their children's lives. Parents also reflected upon their children's potential partners and the consequences of such alliances, especially in terms of the dilution or reinforcement of ethnic minority heritage. For some parents, this was a difficult and emotional conversation to have. Many of the participants spoke about their own family's role in the evolving make-up of British society—that is, they framed change around racial mixture by talking about themselves and their children as being at the forefront of a contemporary Britain, in which there is a great deal of flux surrounding the meanings and dynamics of racial and ethnic boundaries.

Lastly, I review the key findings of this study, many of which point to the growing normality of mixing and mixedness. This conclusion also considers the extent to which the lives of multiracial people in Britain mirror or differ from, those of multiracial people in the United States, and whether theorizing based upon the United States, including dominant understandings about racism and racial hierarchies there, are applicable to contemporary Britain.

1

Multiracial People as Parents

An Overview of Research on Multiracial People

In 2001, David Parker and I observed that "the topic of 'mixed race' can bring out the worst in people."[1] What we meant by this tart remark was that the topic tended to elicit polarized views, so that while some regarded mixed people and "mixing" as hugely problematic, others saw it as the answer to many of our social ills. The current growth in academic writings and forms of popular culture concerning multiracial people demonstrate that we have reached a key juncture in how scholars and the wider society think about and represent multiracial people and their families. In fact, as Jayne Ifekwunigwe observes, we have witnessed three different "ages" of multiracial thinking and discourse, starting with the "Age of Pathology," then going on to the "Age of Celebration," and now to the "Age of Critique," in which much of the recent scholarship in the twenty-first century has adopted a more critical and skeptical stance toward multiracial status, identifications, and experiences. [2]

Earlier scholarship about multiracial people tended to depict such individuals as leading a difficult in-between, "marginal man" existence, marked by emotional and psychological insecurity.[3] Through much of the early to middle twentieth century, anxieties about racial mixing sat uneasily with proclamations about racial equality and justice in the civil rights movement. This is evident in many cultural representations (both in literary and cinematic forms) of the tragic mulatto, who was typically portrayed as someone who suffered bodily disharmony and psychological instability.[4] High rates in the dissolution of interracial unions, as well as the disproportionate numbers of mixed Black/White children in foster care, also comprised key parts of the negative discourse surrounding "mixing" and mixed people.[5]

Countering the pathologizing discourses about mixing, and growing out of the multiracial movement spearheaded by groups on American college campuses, a new generation of scholars, many multiracial themselves, adopted a more celebratory stance toward their multiracial backgrounds, though much of this literature also highlighted the personal difficulties and experiences associated with being mixed.[6] Emblematic of this kind of defiant and celebratory stance are the volumes edited by Maria Root.[7] Along with her theorizing on multiracial identity development, the pioneering work of historian Paul Spickard has been important in shaping much of subsequent work.[8] Rather than elaborating a staged model of identity development in multiracial individuals,[9] Root proposes that multiracial people can adopt four modes of "border crossing," which have been subsequently adapted by many scholars. They are "having *both* feet in *both* groups"; "the shifting of foreground and background as one crosses between and among social contexts defined by race and ethnicity"; "one decisively sits on the border"; and "one creates a home in one 'camp' for an extended period of time and makes forays into other camps from time to time."[10] Furthermore, she outlines a "bill of rights for racially mixed people," in which mixed individuals are urged to assert any identification they wish, regardless of other people's challenges to such claims.[11] As in other British research on mixedness and mixing, this book takes neither a negative nor celebratory stance toward interracial unions and multiracial people.[12] In fact, various scholars have argued that normative stances on mixing are misplaced, as well as being a dead-end in terms of advancing our understanding of this growing phenomenon.[13]

One immediate challenge in any study of multiracial people is the huge diversity contained within such a category, even when we limit our focus to one specific country. Furthermore, where do we situate multiracial people in racially stratified societies, which are usually understood to be comprised of monoracial groups? Are multiracial people in majority White countries more like White people or more like minority people in terms of their social experiences? Interestingly, a recent Pew survey of multiracial Americans found that those with Black ancestry tend to have a set of experiences and social interactions that "are much more closely aligned with the black community," while those with Asian ancestry "feel more closely connected to whites than to Asians."[14] Given the numerous studies of multiracial people in the United States—a country with a very distinctive racial history—it is imperative that the status and experiences of multiracial people in other countries, such as Britain, be explored.

Interracial Couples and the Racial Identification of Multiracial Children

The contentious issue of how multiracial people are identified (vis-à-vis others in a racially stratified society), along with the social and political implications of such identifications, has constituted a key focus of research for many American scholars of interracial unions and multiracial people. A great deal of the US literature on multiracial people has looked at census data (or other large national surveys) and investigated how interracial couples—that is, those consisting of partners with different monoracial backgrounds—have racially identified their multiracial children.[15] Generally speaking, these studies found that Black/White interracial couples in the United States were more likely to identify their children with their minority race (Black) than were Asian/White, Latino/White, and Native American/White couples, who racially classified their multiracial children in more varied ways.[16]

Now, however, some analysts in the United States have found that Black/White interracial couples are less constrained in classifying their multiracial children solely as "Black," and conclude that there has been a gradual weakening of the "one drop rule" of hypodescent in the United States,[17] though others report the continuing strength of the "one drop rule" for Black and part-Black people.[18] In her study of intermarried Black and White couples and their racial identification of their children, Wendy Roth found that most of these couples rejected the "one drop rule," and instead designated a multiracial category for their children.[19] Roth argues that any divergence from the norm to classify multiracial Black/White children as Black is significant because of the historical strength of such a norm.[20] Furthermore, Carolyn Liebler's recent analysis of how the children of many types of interracial unions in the United States (between 1960 and 2010) are categorized points to the growing salience of both multiracial Asian and multiracial Black as categories that are used in mixed families and in the wider society.[21]

While they do not explicitly say so, many of these studies imply that there is likely to be a correspondence between how parents in interracial unions racially see their children (identification) with how these children will come to see themselves over time (identity). Parents are indisputably one of the most fundamental influences on how multiracial children will identify, racially and ethnically, but children's sense of themselves cannot be automatically presumed or read off of how parents designate them on census or other large survey forms.[22] As cogently articulated by Steven Holloway and his colleagues, "The racial claims of parents on behalf of their multiracial children . . . reflect, if only imperfectly, their understanding of who their children are racially, as well as who they may want their children to become racially."[23] The exploration of who multiracial people want their children to become is central to this book.

Many studies employing census data and other large data sets in the United States have also regarded the question of how parents identify their multiracial children as an important snapshot of the racial landscape and a revealing indicator of the continuing salience of racial boundaries and differential racial privileges. For instance, David Brunsma argues that there is emerging evidence of a "reverse hypo-descent" process occurring in how multiracial children are being racially labelled—at least for some kinds of mixed households.[24] Given the opportunity, some interracial couples engage in what Charles Gallagher has called "racial redistricting" in order both to distance their multiracial children from a stigmatized minority status and to reap the benefits of a closer proximity to Whiteness.[25] Kerry Ann Rockquemore and Patricia Arend contend that the fact that some multiracial people in the United States are now identifying as White is evidence of "an expansion of the rules of whiteness that reduce the absolute need for 'racial purity,' and instead imply socioeconomic standards and cultural assimilation as the price of admission."[26] Furthermore, in a study linking changes in racial classification (by others) and racial identification with social stratification processes, Aliya Saperstein and Andrew Penner found that as individuals experienced forms of upward mobility, they were more likely to be "whitened" by others and to whiten their own identifications, and that as some experienced unemployment or were incarcerated, the opposite was true, and they were more likely to "darken" their identifications (or be seen as more Black by others).[27]

Despite the significant number of studies of how interracial couples racially identify their children, researchers have been able only to speculate about *why* parents identify their multiracial children in particular ways. As David Brunsma points out, "We need to know much more about what these identification processes mean for these parents of mixed-race children. It may be, as I suggest, that they are seeing the structure of resource distribution, the racialized and pigmentized racial hierarchy, and the link between the two, and beginning to distance their children from the bottom of that hierarchy."[28] While such motivations on the part of parents of multiracial children cannot be discounted, they may constitute only *part of the explanation* for how and why parents identify and socialize their children in particular ways. Some of these studies can adopt an overly narrow and instrumental understanding of how parents in interracial unions think about and weigh up choices about their children. A further difficulty with studies that focus on how parents racially identify their mixed children is that there is no information about who fills in the census forms or whether the racial designation of children is discussed or in any way negotiated among family members. Families that have members with attachments to multiple and different ethnic or racial groups may experience differences and even conflicts in relation to the identification and socialization of their children.[29] While various US studies have documented the identification of multiracial children on official forms, we still know very little about how multiracial children are brought up in their families.

Raising Multiracial Children

While a number of studies of multiracial children have centered on parents' ability to foster racial awareness, the vast majority of these studies have addressed the experiences of Black/White multiracial children.[30] In Britain, a growing body of work has examined whether White mothers are equipped to raise their mixed Black/White children so that they will have both a positive sense of self and the ability to cope with the negative racial encounters they will almost certainly experience at various points in their lives.[31] But even among parents who are, broadly speaking, racially conscious, the particular ways in which they teach their children and introduce them to the outer world is bound to differ in a variety of ways. According to Wendy Roth: "While some parents see their children as Black and view their role as teaching them how to form a positive Black identity, others see their role as teaching them life skills that transcend racial issues."[32]

In addition to fostering racial awareness, analysts have also addressed broader developmental issues for multiracial individuals. For instance, Kerry Ann Rockquemore and Tracey Laszloffy emphasize the importance of not denying any one part of their ethnic and racial heritage if multiracial children are to develop a healthy sense of self, regardless of how they may identify themselves to others.[33] One key concern for parents of multiracial children is their overall well-being in light of various possible scenarios that could negatively impact their adjustment, such as a discrepancy between asserted racial identification and others' racial assignment of them.[34] On the whole, most studies have found no *major* disadvantages in well-being associated with a multiracial background;

nor are the experiences of multiracial people necessarily different from those of monoracial minority groups.[35]

Some of this literature shares a great deal in common with studies of transracial adoption (TRA) and fostering, which explicitly address concerns about parents' ability to support racial awareness and cultural and ethnic socialization for such children and to develop what Elizabeth Vonk and Richard Massatti refer to as "cultural competence" on the part of adoptive (White) parents.[36]

Thus, while many studies of multiracial children have addressed various developmental concerns, few studies about the parenting of multiracial children have investigated issues around ethnic and cultural transmission in tandem with parents' efforts to foster racial awareness.[37] One important British study of 35 "mixed-parent couples" carried out by Chamion Caballero, Rosalind Edwards, and Shuby Puthussery found that these couples could be "mixed" in terms of racial, ethnic, and/or religious differences.[38] These families could thus vary considerably in terms of the degree to which religion, ethnicity, and race matter (or not), and we cannot presume that "race" is necessarily the most salient factor for multiracial people and their families.[39] Furthermore, there are multiple sites at which "mixing" is occurring and is recognized: "Multiraciality is an emergent form of diversity that is increasingly visible at the scales of the body, the family, and the neighbourhood."[40]

Growth in Numbers of Mixed People in Britain

In Britain, the terms "mixed race" and "mixed" (as opposed to "multiracial," which is more common in the United States) are now increasingly commonplace in popular culture, government, and the multitude of organizations we inhabit in our daily lives. Since the time when "Mixed" was first offered as an option in the ethnicity question in the 2001 England and Wales census, Britain's recognition of, and interest in, mixed people has not abated. In the 2011 census, mixed people were estimated to be about 2.2 percent of the population, as opposed to about 1.2 percent in 2001, with White and Black Caribbean mixed people comprising the largest subgroup (see Table 1.1).[41] However, what we mean by "mixed race" (that is, who counts as mixed race) and our understanding of mixed people's varied identifications and experiences are still quite nascent in the British context.[42] The official estimate of 2.2 percent in the 2011 census is almost certainly an under-count because some individuals who are mixed by parentage may still choose a single ethnic box, and the same is true of some parents of mixed children, who may categorize them in relation to one ethnic or racial background.[43] In other words, the census figure is a measure of how people identify themselves, not a measure of how many people are actually the children of interracial unions.[44]

TABLE 1.1: Ethnic Groups, England and Wales, 2011

White	86% (of which 80.5% were White British)
Asian/Asian British	7.5%
Black/African/Caribbean/Black British	3.3%
Mixed/Multiple ethnic groups	2.2%
Other ethnic group	1.0%

Source: Ethnicity and National Identity in England and Wales 2011, ONS

As this book will illustrate, the ways in which parents think about ethnic and racial categories and how they apply to their children can be highly varied. The racial/ethnic terms and classifications used to represent the "multiracial" or "mixed-race" population vary across individuals, regions, government agencies, and the wider society.[45] Furthermore, people's understandings of multiracial status and terminology is often messier than conceived by official bodies. For instance, in Britain, the Office for National Statistics (ONS) employs an exact two-group combination, which effectively limits the understanding of mixed status to those who are *first-generation* mixed (someone who had "single race" parents of two distinct races).[46] However, research shows that around a fifth of those identifying as mixed race choose (unprompted) to name three or more constituent groups.[47] Clearly, research on multiracial people needs to adopt a more nuanced understanding of how people understand their mixedness and of who counts as mixed.

The mixed population is predicted to grow very quickly in the coming decades, continuing a trend of increased demographic diversity in Britain in the last several decades.[48] For instance, one model predicts annual growth rates of 3.82 percent in Britain for the years 2006 to 2032.[49] In the United States, according to the US Census Bureau, the multiracial population is predicted to triple by 2060.[50] In response to the ethnicity question posed in the England and Wales census, those who chose "White" as their ethnic group decreased from 94 percent in 1991 to 86 percent in 2011. This shows that in the last two decades, England and Wales have become more ethnically diverse (at least in terms of how people regard their ethnicities), and this is reflected in the way in which the ONS has gathered data about ethnic background: Since 1991 the number of tick boxes for ethnicity has grown from 9 in 1991 (when there was no "Mixed" option) to 18 in the 2011 census (see Box 1.1).

Along with this increase in mixed people and households and reflecting their increasing prominence in the British media and in public policies, studies of mixed-race people and families in Britain have also grown considerably. The early research of Susan Benson and Ann Wilson were important in mapping the distinctive experiences of Black/White mixed households and children.[51] Since then, a number of studies have explored the racial identifications and understandings of mixed people and their families.[52] Also, a growing number of studies have investigated the thoughts and experiences of mixed children in the context of family lives and relationships.[53] More recently, Peter Aspinall and I carried out a study of mixed young people in higher education, in which mixed people with disparate ethnic "mixes" provided detailed accounts of their identities and experiences.[54]

Yet, we still know very little about the socioeconomic backgrounds and family lives of the emergent and increasingly diverse multiracial population in Britain. Data from the Millenium Cohort Study, a multi-

Box 1.1: England and Wales 2011 Census: Ethnic Group Question
What is your ethnic group?

→ Choose one section from A to E, then tick one box to best describe your ethnic group or background

A *White*
- ☐ English/Welsh/Scottish/Northern Irish/British
- ☐ Irish
- ☐ Gypsy or Irish Traveler
- ☐ Any other White background, write in:

_____

B *Mixed/multiple ethnic groups*
- ☐ White and Black Caribbean
- ☐ White and Black African
- ☐ White and Asian
- ☐ Any other Mixed/multiple ethnic background, write in:

_____

C *Asian/Asian British*
- ☐ Indian
- ☐ Pakistani
- ☐ Bangladeshi
- ☐ Chinese
- ☐ Any other Asian background, write in:

_____

D *Black/African/Caribbean/Black British*
- ☐ African
- ☐ Caribbean
- ☐ Any other Black/African/Caribbean background, write in:

_____

E *Other ethnic group*
- ☐ Arab
- ☐ Any other ethnic group, write in:

_____

disciplinary, longitudinal research project following the lives of around 19,000 children born in the United Kingdom in 2000–2001, suggests that mixed children are in families with relative socioeconomic advantage, thus countering stereotypical images of mixed children born to, and raised by, uneducated and underprivileged parents.[55] When we disaggregate the mixed population, we find that mixed people of disparate ethnic and racial ancestries occupy varied class positions and trajectories; in fact, some question the validity of conceiving of multiracial people as a group.[56]

Black Caribbean/White mixed people in Britain appear to have a distinctive set of experiences, in relation to other types of mixed people in Britain. For instance, mixed children (many of Black/White ancestry) are disproportionately likely to be placed in foster care.[57] Furthermore, Black Caribbeans are said to be following an "Irish pattern of integration," in that their partners are often working-class White Britons. This parallel also suggests that Black Caribbeans will eventually be "fully absorbed into the British population."[58] In comparison with Black Caribbeans, Britons of Indian ancestry have been slower to partner with White Britons; when they have, they have done so along "Jewish, rather than Irish, lines," such that those with higher degrees are more likely to partner with White Britons.[59]

Conceptualizing and Measuring the Multiracial Population

Given the dominance of US studies of multiracial people, which are usually based upon the historically specific experiences of Black/White people, we need to investigate the ways in which "mixture" has played out in other societies.[60] While many countries around the world recognize and categorize some forms of mixed ancestry, they do so in quite different ways and employ a variety of terms (and concepts) such as ancestry, race, ethnicity, nationality, indigenous group, and cultural group.[61] Furthermore, analysts have begun to document the ways in which countries do and do not enumerate ethnic and racial difference and how these practices are driven by a host of historical, political, and social factors specific to each society.[62] For example, the use of "race" in North American and Caribbean "New World" societies has been fundamentally shaped by the histories of slavery in those societies.

For some decades, social scientists have explored the status and experiences of multiracial people in countries such as Brazil[63] and Mexico.[64] More recently, studies of mixed people and families in Scandinavian and less studied European societies,[65] Canada,[66] and Australia and New Zealand,[67] have also been growing, as has attention to the multiethnic and multiracial individuals in East Asian societies such as Japan.[68] All of these studies demonstrate the importance of specific historical and regional understandings of difference and the formation of racial regimes.

While some of the insights and findings from studies of multiracial people in the United States are valuable and even applicable to other countries such as Britain, the history of race and colonization in the United States is highly distinctive, and in particular the persistent Black/White racial divide is unlike the kinds of racial divides that are emerging in Britain. In comparison with the United States, Black/White intermarriage is relatively high and increasingly common in Britain. In an analysis of the Labour Force Survey, a quarterly survey that captures statistics on employment and household characteristics, nearly half of Black Caribbean men *in a partnership* were partnered (marrying or cohabiting) with someone of a different ethnic group (as were about one third of Black Caribbean women), while 39 percent of Chinese women in a partnership had a partner from a different ethnic group.[69] Such "interethnic partnerships" may not necessarily be interracial unions, but many of them do involve White partners.

Given the increasing rates of interracial unions for South Asian and East Asian origin people in Britain, their experiences clearly need further investigation. The specific ethnic "mix" of multiracial people is known to shape their social experiences and the ways in which they identify themselves and their children.[70] Thus a varied sample of mixed participants in Britain is crucial. But moving beyond the binary of Black/White is perhaps easier said than done, as this duality represents the archetype of racial difference.[71] Crucial to moving beyond this binary, also, is the importance of recognizing the degree of diversity within ethnic groups that are typically presumed to "contain" individuals with a great deal in common.[72] What Rogers Brubaker has called "groupism" is highly problematic, and so while this book employs categories that point to distinct types of mixed people, such as South Asian/White or Black/White people, it does not presume a homogeneity of experience or interests.[73]

Furthermore, as studies of multiracial people and their family lives continue to grow, we need a better understanding of the roles of their partners, particularly in terms of their contributions to childrearing and family life more generally. While this book draws specifically on surveys and interviews with a multiracial participant in each household, these interviews yielded rich information about the roles of their partners and the ways in which our participants interacted with them. According to the Office for National Statistics, "mixed" people are the most likely to be married to someone "outside their ethnic group"—that is, to someone who is not "mixed" (in Britain, most mixed people are partnered with White Britons).[74] However, mixed people in Britain are often married to "someone from a related ethnic group"—that is, many mixed people have partners with whom they share some ethnic overlap (such as a shared White or Black ancestry).[75]

Much of the US literature on mixed people emphasizes the privileges of potentially passing as White or of the racially ambiguous status occupied by the growing numbers of part Asian and part Latino Americans.[76] While the privileges of a White appearance are indisputable in many social settings,[77] there are few investigations of how multiracial people who may be seen as White (or are seen as racially ambiguous by others) or who are the children of one or more multiracial parents may feel about the process of ethnic and racial "dilution."[78] In Britain, we cannot assume (as suggested in much of the US literature) that most (first- or second-generation) multiracial people will automatically want to upgrade to Whiteness if given the chance to do so.

In many respects, in the early twenty-first century, academic (and popular) attention to multiracial people is segueing into questions about how they may identify, affiliate, and belong in relation to their ethnic minority ancestries, as many multiracial people partner with White individuals. In contrast to historical concerns about how mixed people might "pass" in order to claim White privilege, growing scholarship also addresses the thorny questions of whether and how multiracial people may wish (and be able) to retain a link with their minority ancestries.[79]

Interestingly, in comparison with the continuing emphasis upon the reality of race and racial difference in US scholarship, many leading British scholars on race have tended to articulate arguments about the need to transcend race and racial language and thinking and to rethink existing racial frames altogether (though they recognize the persistence of ethnic and racial prejudice and discrimination in various forms). Some, such as Suki Ali, have argued for the adoption of a "deconstructive, post-race analysis" in the study of mixed people and interethnic co-mingling,[80] while Kevin Hylton and colleagues have fostered debate about critical race theory in relation to the multiracial population in Britain.[81] And on the European continent, the language and notion of race is assiduously avoided in many European countries.[82]

Central to many concerns about the study of mixed-race or multiracial people has been the contention that to study mixed race, one inevitably reifies a notion of a pure, unsullied "race"; Michael Banton has tirelessly argued against the use of "mixed race" and has advocated the use of "mixed origin" instead as the less problematic alternative.[83] In ongoing debates about the most appropriate (or least problematic) terminology, others, like Minelle Mahtani and April Moreno, have argued that "mixed race" can imply the contamination of Whiteness, and can obscure other kinds of "mixture" that do not involve a White ancestor.[84] Despite the appeal of post-racial aspirations, we still need a vocabulary to talk about people who are the children of unions that are deemed interracial, and in this book I use "mixed race," "mixed," and "multiracial" interchangeably, knowing that these terms are subject to continuing debate.

Multiracial People and Their Children—A Generation Farther Down

Studies using census data and other large-scale data sets to investigate how parents identify their multiracial children tend to presume a great deal about how parents make choices about the identification of their children. Since the identification of multiracial children in large scale surveys (through the nomination of specific racial categories) can tell us only so much, it is crucial that we distinguish the classification of children on official forms from the ways in which parents see, and raise, their children. As discussed in this book, a complex array of factors shape intergenerational transmission of ethnic and racial identities and the ways in which parents raise their children. These factors include the relative strength or weakness of the minority parent's identification with his or her minority heritage; his or her experiences of prejudice and discrimination; the ethnic and racial backgrounds of his or her partner; the geographical location of such families and the presence of coethnics (and other ethnic minority people); and contact with extended family members such as grandparents who may speak a language other than English.[85] Furthermore, the processes underlying how and why parents identify and raise their children in the ways they do are far from straightforward and can involve uncertainties, nuances and ambiguities—none of which can be captured through large-scale survey tick boxes.

Looking down a generation, how might multiracial parents see the racial identification and socialization of their children? How does their being multiracial influence the racial designation of their own children? By the logic of US studies above, multiracial parents should designate their children in relation to the most racially privileged group, as opposed to their minority designation. But is this the case for multiracial people in Britain? While the debates about multiracial status in the United States have some resonance, I argue that the ways in which the multiracial people in this study think and talk about their life experiences, and their children suggest a distinctive set of experiences for multiracial people in Britain.

A generational shift is required in our study of multiracial people and their experiences. In Britain, as in the United States, there are now multigeneration multiracial people, whose parents and/or grandparents are multiracial themselves.[86] Thus, it is useful to differentiate between people who are *immediately* mixed, or those who regard their parents as being of different races, from people who are more *remotely* mixed, or those whose "mixture" is derived from farther up the family tree, for instance, through grandparents or even more distant ancestors.[87]

The 2015 Pew survey of multiracial Americans employs a definition of "multiracial" that explicitly refers to the racial backgrounds of respondents' parents *and* grandparents. So even respondents who may have mostly White ancestry in their family tree can be counted as "multiracial" if a parent or grandparent was either in an interracial union or had multiracial ancestry.

> Included in our definition of multiracial adults are 1) those who select two or more races for themselves; 2) those who do not select two or more races for themselves but report that at least one of their parents was not the same race as the one they selected for themselves, or select at least two or more races for at least one of their biological parents; 3) respondents who do not fit the definition of "multiracial" based on their own or their parents' racial background, but indicate that at least one of their grandparents was not the same race as themselves or their parents, or select two or more races for their grandparents.[88]

What are the implications of how we understand and measure multiracial status down the generational pipeline? For one, generational differences in the locus of mixture may be significant for how multiracial people identify and raise their children. While there has been growing attention to the rich and varied histories of interracial relationships and multiracial people and communities in Britain, we still know very little about *multiracial people as adults and as parents* in contemporary Britain. As in the Pew survey definition of "multiracial," this book includes multiracial participants who are either first-generation mixed (the offspring of two parents who are of disparate races), or less commonly, second-generation mixed (the offspring of at least one parent who is multiracial).

Just as we cannot generalize about mixed people as a group, which presumes shared experiences and commonalities, so we cannot generalize about their approach to parenting their children. Nevertheless, some research suggests that multiracial people are particularly attune to certain issues, stemming from their status as multiracial, as opposed to monoracial, individuals. For instance, social psychologists have claimed that mixed people are more aware of the fact that race and racial difference are socially constructed than are monoracial people.[89] Once we move down a generation, how may multiracial people differ as parents (as opposed to parents in interracial unions)?[90] Being raised and socialized by two racially disparate parents is likely to be a different experience to growing up in a household with a multiracial parent.[91]

While there is growing evidence that racial identification is becoming gradually less prescriptive, much of the literature (especially studies based on large survey data) has tended to overlook the possibility that, with generational (and genealogical) distance, mixed people are not always knowledgeable about their parents' (and grandparents') ancestries and that, like most others, they may emphasize only selected aspects of their ancestry.[92] Such knowledge of ancestors may be even more elusive in the case of families with "mixing," particularly given the taboo surrounding mixed unions that existed until very recently; thus there is real scope for unknown, or rewritten family narratives about the actual ethnic and racial backgrounds of family members.

With each generational remove in their family trees, information about ancestors is increasingly likely to be lost or indeterminate.[93] In a recent British study, Peter Aspinall and I found that, on the whole, the ethnic and racial backgrounds of ancestors higher up the family tree (that is, more distant) were less meaningful to mixed-race young people than those of (genealogically closer) relatives such as parents and grandparents.[94] In this book, the study participants possessed variable amounts of interest and knowledge about their family lineages. Because so much of extant literature has focused only on the first-generation progeny of interracial unions, the experiences and identifications of second- (or even third-) generation mixed people are still unchartered territory.

2

How Do Multiracial People Identify Their Children?

Since multiracial people are, by definition, more than one race, how do they think about and choose the ways in which they identify their children, and what do these choices mean? Multiracial people can identify themselves in different ways. For example, some who may know of a minority grandparent or (minority ancestry further back) may not consider themselves mixed, while others identify as such, despite this generational remove.[1] One common convention for first-generation mixed people (individuals with two distinct single-race parents, such as Black and White, or East Asian and White) has been to employ the language of fractions and to say that they are half X, and half Y. But if one parent is multiracial (or if both are), the question of how his or her (or their) own children should be seen becomes far from straightforward, because there is no established convention for how second-generation mixed people should be identified.

As David Skinner has noted, in Britain, ethnic and racial categories "have become part of the fabric of everyday life as citizens are expected to locate themselves within official systems of categorization not only via the national census but through 'ethnic monitoring' in employment, education, policing and the provision of many public services."[2] Yet how multiracial individuals (as parents) fill in such forms and what their identifications of their children may reveal are still largely unknown.[3] Furthermore, the taken-for-grantedness of racial categories and terms is increasingly contested in many contemporary contexts.[4]

In one of the only studies focused *specifically* on multiracial people and their children in the United States, Jenifer Bratter investigates to what extent "multiracial" as a parental identity is associated with classifying a child as multiracial across families with four types of interracial parents.[5] Given that there are no clear conventions for how to racially identify children with one or more multiracial parents, Bratter poses the following questions through this example: "A biracial woman of White and Asian background and her White partner clearly have a White racial background in common. In this instance, is it appropriate to consider the child 'multiracial' or is 'White' the more appropriate label, since it is the most prevalent racial background? Should we consider children of multiracial parents to be multiracial if both parents have one race in common?"[6] As discussed below, the uncertainty about how multiracial people should identify their children was also often evident among the British multiracial parents in this study.

According to Bratter, one key finding is that the impact of being a multiracial parent (on classifying their children) depended on whether or not the two parents' racial backgrounds overlapped.[7] In one analysis using US census data, Bratter focused on how partially Black parents classified their children, and in particular whether they classified their children as "Black."[8] While parents with a shared White background did not make the identification of their children as White very likely (though this was not a tiny proportion either),[9] Bratter found that a racial overlap of Black heritage resulted in the *likelihood* that such a couple would classify their child as solely Black. But when a partially Black parent had a spouse of any other race (other than Black), there was virtually no chance that such a couple would identify their child as solely Black. Interestingly, even a shared Black heritage *did not guarantee* that parents would identify their child as monoracially Black, since about one third of such families classified their children as "multiracial." Bratter also found that over 85 percent of families with *two* partially Black multiracial parents identified their children with multiple races. Bratter concludes that there is strong evidence that a "multiracial" classification is employed and recognized in households with a multiracial parent, which suggests a waning of the "one drop rule" in relation to partially Black people in the United States.

While large, survey-based studies in the United States have been valuable in revealing the patterns in how interracial couples identify their children, as has Bratter's study of multiracial parents, they cannot explain the reasons *why* multiracial children are labeled and identified in particular ways or what such choices on survey forms actually mean in terms of how multiracial parents raise their children. Only a qualitative approach can capture a fuller understanding of why parents identify their children in the ways they do—an understanding that includes a consideration of children's physical appearances and the ways in which parents' own racialized experiences may inform the ways they view their children. Looking at a generation farther down, at the *children* of such interracial unions, analysts have yet to investigate the choices that multiracial people make, *as parents*, in the identification of their own children.

All parents, but in particular non-White parents, rely upon a racial worldview to navigate potentially hostile encounters and environments for their children.[10] Do multiracial parents want to encourage a particular racial identification (such as "mixed") or stance toward their minority or White ancestries in their children? As Jenifer Bratter and Holly Heard have asked: "Just as mothers and fathers invest in their child's well-being through their parenting, might they also 'invest' in their child's identity?"[11] While many parents (in general) may want their children to develop some appreciation of their family heritage, the issue of parents' (and grandparents') ethnic and racial backgrounds and what they mean (if anything at all) may be of particular interest to or concern for multiracial people, especially those who become parents.

This question of how multiracial people identify their children is of wider social and political importance not only because the answers to this question may reveal different ethnic options for multiracial people, but also because they provide a fuller understanding of how and whether ethnic and racial difference may or may not continue to matter now and in the future as multiracial people and households grow in number.[12] Clearly, the category of "multiracial" (or "mixed") is populated by a highly diverse population, and as mixed people form unions and have children (and grandchildren), it becomes increasingly important to specify the generational locus of mixture and to examine whether there is a generational "tipping point" at which minority heritage is regarded as of little or no significance.

This chapter aims to unpack what multiracial parents' classifications of their children mean and how they are made. In addition to the racial background of the multiracial parent's spouse (and potential racial overlap), how might the physical appearance of children, along with the parents' own upbringing and life experiences, influence their decisions about the identifications of their children? By comparing disparate types of multiracial people, we are able to explore whether mixed people of varied racial ancestries differ in the identification of their children. In this chapter, I argue that parents' racial identifications of their children should be understood in terms of how multiracial parents see (and wish to see) their children—but that the basis upon which they identify their children can differ among parents.

Findings

Rather than being offered a choice of close-ended categories, our participants were asked about how they would identify their children on official forms and why. We then coded their open-ended responses into the above categories. As we will see below, unlike the neatness of "tick boxes" on surveys and forms, many participants' responses to this question were imbued with ambivalence and/or uncertainty. Furthermore, it was not uncommon for participants to express some weariness about the ubiquity of ethnic monitoring forms in various spheres of their lives.

Most participants were able to choose a category for their children and explain their choices. The main finding is the large number of parents (across all multiracial "types") who chose a "mixed" designation for their children. It is striking that while 40 (of 62) parents identified their children as mixed, and 14 identified their children as White/White

TABLE 2.1: How Participants Classified Their Children on Official Forms

Mixed/multiple ethnic group	40 (65%)
White	14 (23%)
Monoracial minority group	0 (0%)
Refuse to categorize	5 (8 %)
I can't say / I don't know	3 (4 %)
TOTAL	62 (100%)

British, *none* chose a monoracial minority category, such as "Asian" or "Black" in identifying their children. It is perhaps not surprising that a single minority race was not chosen by the few participants who had minority partners with whom they did *not* share any ancestry. But I had expected that *some* of those participants who shared a minority racial background with their partner, such as a Black/White person partnered with a Black person, might identify their children in relation to that shared race.[13]

Those Who Chose "Mixed"

Of the 40 participants who classified their children as "Mixed-multiple ethnic group," the majority of these (25) were Black/White participants, with 8 South Asian/White and 7 East Asian/White. As discussed above, none of our participants identified their children in terms of a single minority category, such as Black. Even those participants with a minority race in common with their partners said that they would classify their children as mixed, as opposed to their shared monoracial minority race, such as Black or South Asian.

One participant, Victor (second-generation mixed Black/White, 39), had a White Irish mother and a mixed Black Caribbean/White father. Victor had a child with his Black African partner, and he revealed that it was very important to him that his son was raised with an appreciation of and pride in his Black Caribbean and Black African heritages. It was evident that Victor felt a strong attachment to his Black ancestry and to other Black people. He reported that he and his wife had considered identifying their son as Black on official forms, given their shared Black ancestry, but after some discussion, they had decided that a multiracial designation was most appropriate.

> It's a strange one because it's come up a few times. I think it would be "mixed-race African." These forms are quite strange because sometimes you don't have a box. And obviously I'm not White. We've talked about it a few times [he and his wife]. And we've even wondered if we'd put Black in there, but then there's that business in my heritage, on my [White Irish] mum's side. So we usually put "mixed-race Black African."

Victor was close to and had frequent contact with his White Irish mother, who often looked after his son. Therefore, Victor was uncomfortable about using a monoracial designation for his son, as it would seem to completely omit his White mother (and his mixed father's White ancestry) from his lineage. In this case, racial overlap (of their Black ancestry) was not a sufficient basis for Victor and his wife to identify their son as solely Black—though another couple with the same ethnic and racial ancestries between them might, of course, have chosen Black.

Louise (Black/White, 44) had a son with her now ex-partner, who was Black Jamaican (but with one White grandmother), and she, too, considered herself and her son to be "mixed," even though her son's father was mostly Black. She urged her son Jake to say he was mixed and to take pride in his mixed background. As Louise noted, "he has a White grandmother [mother's side] and a White great-grandmother [father's side]":

> I was more than adamant. "You are Irish-Jamaican, if anyone asks you, you're Irish-Jamaican, that is what you are, don't let anybody." Because I've had people [say] that I can't be, I've had people tell me "no, you're not," so I think that's where my adamance [sic] comes from, I won't have that taken away from him, in the way that people tried to take it away from me.

This insistence upon her son as mixed derived from her own experiences of being denied such recognition, often by well-meaning "liberals" who were being "politically correct":

I remember having a conversation about this many years ago with a young lad who was mixed race. And people were denying our conversation, they were denying the contents of our conversation. "No, it doesn't matter, mixed race doesn't matter, there's not [sic] such things as 'race' anyway." All this kind of thing. . . . And it's just like, if it was just us, just myself on a desert island, with my parents, it wouldn't be an issue, the only thing that makes it an issue is that when you go into a society that really is partisan along race lines, or very narrowly defined race lines, you suddenly realize that you're an issue for everybody else. You're an issue for the racists, you're an issue for some very right-on people . . . who somehow want me to identify as Black and not mixed race, being mixed race to them is problematic.

Furthermore, for Louise, the assertion of her (and her son's) mixedness was of fundamental importance to her because she did not feel socially or culturally "Black":

But I can't be culturally black, I didn't grow up around black people. I grew up around white people, I went to school with mainly white people. I didn't have black friends until I was in my twenties. So that's really . . . it's very difficult to be culturally something. . . . I find it very difficult to talk race or culture, or identity, to people who are from the same area that their parents are from, grandparents, great-grandparents. . . . They've had no challenges to that identity. They've always been from [a part of London], they've always been from wherever, here. And they've never had to question it, they've never had to explain it, or express it—it just is. But when it's so different, two immigrants [her parents] but from different cultures, different continents, growing up in a rather, at times, hostile environment, you have to learn to run the gamut.

These cases suggest that participants who had children with partners with a shared minority ancestry, such as Victor and Louise, could have different motivations for designating their children as mixed. A principled insistence upon recognizing all aspects of one's lineage was evident in these accounts—though Victor's and Louise's life experiences and racial identifications differed. While Victor identified as a mixed person with a strong affiliation with his Black ancestry, Louise identified as a mixed person who felt strongly English. These examples support Bratter's finding (discussed above) that a (Black) racial overlap among the households she studied in the United States did not guarantee that a child would be identified as monoracially Black.[14]

For participants who had *White* partners (46 of 62), the majority of such participants (32 of 46) reported that their children would be identified as mixed—regardless of their physical appearance and the fact that their children were another generation removed from their minority ancestry. This identification of their children as multiracial raised a variety of themes and concerns about the significance of family lineage, the generational locus of mixture, and the legitimacy of recognizing blood quantum and racial fractions. For example, when asked about how she would identify her children, Amanda (Black/White, 47) reported:

> I'd put mixed, yeah. And I think it's simply about not negating a part of yourself regardless of what you think you look like or what they think, you know, that's what you are . . . if you're subscribing to those forms of classification or categorization.

It was important to Amanda that her children's identifications reflected their multiple racial ancestries, in principle, although she reported that one of her daughters was usually seen as White. Like Amanda, Jonathon (East Asian/White, 42) also refused to let physical appearance determine how he identified his son:

Um . . . I have thought about that . . . and because I don't want identity to be about your visual markers, identity should be about your history, and about the context of where you are now, and all of those things should merge together to form your identity . . . so I regard them as Welsh actually, because they were born in Wales, and I like that, I like the fact that they were born in Wales.

Later in the interview, he elaborated further:

INT: And if you were to choose, say, you're registering at the doctor's surgery, or in school, and you've got to fill out a monitoring form, what would you pick?

JONATHON: Actually the first time we had to do that was a few weeks ago, for Oliver, and we said to each other, "Well, what do we tick for Oliver?" And I couldn't actually . . . I didn't know, it flummoxed me, and I felt awful about it, because you think about the visual markers that obviously don't define people's identity, but he looks very Caucasian, very White, and in the end Faye said, "Well, he's mixed race, of course he's mixed race, it's diluted but he's mixed race." And I said, "You're right, of course he's mixed race," so we ticked mixed race.

Interestingly, both Amanda (discussed earlier) and Jonathon struggled with, and resisted, the dominant "logic" of physical appearance dictating the identification of their children—they defied it, though they knew that others would not necessarily validate the identification of their children as mixed. But at the same time, Jonathon and his wife acknowledged the undeniable fact of "dilution" and their son's White appearance. As Jonathon observed, who his son is should come not only from visual markers, but also from place and historical context, and the fact that his son was born in Wales pleased him, as neither Jonathon nor his wife had any Welsh ancestry.

In response to her son's concern that he wasn't mixed (because he believed that to be mixed, he had to be "half and half"), Sophie (Black/ White, 31) resisted a fractional understanding of what it meant to be multiracial, emphasizing instead the fact that he was "made up of four different countries," without any fractional measures stipulated in relation to them.

> He did say to me, "I'm not half and half." And I said, "Well, that's a good reason why they don't use the word half-caste because if they did then you wouldn't be considered that," and he said, "What would I be considered?" and I said, "Oh, I hate the word Dorian, but in the olden days they used to say 'quarter-caste.' And I used to hate it, I never got worried about half-caste, funnily enough, it didn't bother me, but I didn't like that—a quarter what? So I said to him, "The term 'mixed' is brilliant, because actually that's what you are. You're made up of four different countries."

Some participants with White partners felt rather tentative about claiming a multiracial identification for their children, but nevertheless did so. Like many of the other East Asian/White participants, Diane (53) articulated her concerns about how other people (and in particular other "fully" Chinese or other East Asian people) may regard *her* (or her children's) claim to be part Chinese, due to her uneasiness about being able to demonstrate racial and ethnic authenticity. Given this unease, she was all too aware of how others may challenge her identification of her children as mixed.

> I always feel a bit, not . . . not as if I'm cheating—that's the wrong word— but as if it's not quite how other people would . . . would see it. It's [Chinese heritage] important to me but because I'm very much part of the White culture, I suppose. Not completely but being brought up here . . . I suppose when people get to know me, they . . . they think of me as White, I think. I think they do.

Despite the fact that her Chinese mother's background had not been emphasized in Diane's upbringing, Diane looked racially ambiguous to others. She also reported that her daughter (now in her early twenties) had a somewhat "Chinese" appearance (and had experienced some racial taunting), and felt strongly that her daughter should be designated as multiracial, and not identified as solely White. In this instance, the fact that her daughter did not look wholly White bolstered Diane's conviction that her daughter should be identified as mixed, even though Diane herself had not raised her daughter with the traditional cultural capital associated with being Chinese, such as fluency in a Chinese dialect.

Discourses about physical appearance, ethnic and racial fractions, and dilution were often in play, and many participants with White partners expressed some degree of uncertainty about how they should identify their children. For instance, Jeremy (South Asian/White, 35) said this when asked about how he identified his children on forms:

I think we've talked about it, yeah. Sometimes you do have to put whether you call them "mixed" or whether you'd call them "White." . . . We've chatted about it, but we've never formalized it. Yeah . . . I think I usually put "mixed." But it doesn't seem like, now that they're a smaller fraction that's Indian, it doesn't seem like fair that you'd tick that box or not. Because maybe that's more of a fifty-fifty kind of box [he laughs]. But I often tick that one anyway.

When Claudia (Black/White, 29), whose partner was White British, was asked how she would identify her daughter, she replied:

When she was just born and you had to fill all the sort of doctor's forms and stuff like that it was really weird to think how . . . what box to tick for her. So I ticked the same as me, like White and Black Caribbean. . . . Because that's what she is to a certain . . . but then you just think how far down does it go? Like if she had children with a white person, when would they stop ticking that box? Do you know what I mean? It's a weird . . . it's a weird sort of thing to think about but for me, I was like I can't . . . there's no way that I could sign that the kid [was] completely White so . . . she's not white. So yeah, that's the box we tick.

Clearly, from these excerpts, parents demonstrated an awareness of racial proportions or fractions in their children's make-up, which was one way to think through, or "measure" and justify, their choices. Such awareness of racial fractions was often coupled with varying levels of self-consciousness or anxiety about ethnic and racial authenticity and sadness about cultural dilution and loss.[15] Many parents could feel uncertain about their choices (as conveyed by Claudia above), and were mindful of the possibility that others might not validate the ways in which they regarded their children. Yet the kinds of constraints and concerns that participants perceived regarding the identification of their children could differ for participants of disparate racial mixes. Although it is somewhat ambiguous, Claudia's remark that "There's no way that I could sign that the kid [was] completely White" suggests that she knows that her identification of her (part-Black) daughter as White would not have been accepted by others. Although there is no suggestion that Claudia actually saw her daughter in this way or wanted others to see her as such, she did not consider an assertion of Whiteness on behalf of her daughter as even a remote possibility. Thus participants' concerns about a lack of validation by others or a sense of uncertainty about how to identify their children were tinged with different kinds of unwritten rules and nuances about who could and could not claim membership in particular groups, such as the category "White."

Perhaps not surprisingly, the three respondents with minority partners of a different race (and with no shared heritage) designated their children as multiracial rather than privileging any one race over another. In fact, some parents, like Josh (South Asian/White, 32), identified their children as mixed on forms, but made a point of disavowing the significance of race. Josh's wife, Alicia (Black British, 33), who was at home during the interview, also participated in the interview.

JOSH: I suppose wherever there's a form we choose whatever option is "mixed other," it's the only choice that's applicable to the children.
ALICIA: Yes.

A bit later, in reference to their two children, Alicia said:

ALICIA: But yeah, we don't really . . . I mean, to us they're [their children] just Darren and Amelia, we don't really think about race. But they're a right old mixture aren't they?
JOSH: It would probably be significant to other people who need to tick their boxes, but we're all just individuals anyway.

Here, both Josh and Alicia emphasize the point that their children are first and foremost individuals, who are not reducible to racial "tick boxes" and that in their family lives, there is no recognition of racial difference. In fact, at another point in the interview Josh reported that he and his wife do not think of each other as being of different "races"—rather, it is other people who attribute racial difference to them. Clearly, a disavowal of racial difference was a central narrative in their family culture and affected how they dealt with others' attributions of difference onto them.

Although the majority of participants in this study identified their children as "mixed," the particular meanings of "mixed" were not necessarily uniform. In a few cases, where *both* the participant and her or his partner were multiracial with the same ancestries, participants discussed how their children's heritage should be understood. Both Gemma (32) and her partner were Black/White mixed, and each had a White mother and Black father. At the time of interview, Gemma had a daughter and was expecting another child. Gemma was adamant about her unborn child also being "mixed race":

Well, I say to [partner], 'This child, whatever it looks like [in utero], it is mixed race. Because of . . . both our mums are White, both our dads are Black, so it's the same as us. We're mixed race so . . . it's mixed race.

In the excerpt above, Gemma's understanding of "mixed" refers to the idea of a specific shared mixed ancestry in which she and her partner are both Black and White. She also reflected upon how her children would be seen, since both she and her partner were mixed:

> When people ask about her [daughter's] background, I think she's going to have that as well, because she is like, really fair. So I think people will ask her and she'll have to explain that "my mum's mixed race and then my dad is . . . we call it 'double mix.'" If both your parents are mixed race then you're a "double mix." (She laughs) . . . And there's more double-mix people, little kids now where there never was.

By referring to her daughter's (and unborn baby's) heritage as "double mix," Gemma here signals the importance of recognizing that *both* she and her partner share a *specific* multiracial background—an experience which she suggests is somehow distinctive from that of non-mixed people (or even a household with only one mixed parent).

In some cases, the identification of children as mixed appeared to signal a collective awareness of a shared sense of community with other Black/White mixed people. For instance, among some working-class Black/White participants (especially in certain urban areas), a multigeneration "mixed" identity was clearly emergent or even established alongside others whose parents (and wider social networks) were also known to be Black/White mixed. Dennis (Black/White, 45) expressed such a view:

> Yeah, do you remember what I was speaking to you about, how quite a few of my friends and my peers have got mixed-race kids with a mixed-race woman. The mixed-race children that I've interviewed say that "we are mixed, our mum and dad is [sic] mixed, we are the same as our mum and dad, we just want, we're just the same as two black people or two white people." Even though the original mix had come from a black and a white person their mix is directly from mixed. Everybody that I know like that say [inaudible] he's just mixed race from two mixed race just like his mum and dad.

Like Gemma, Dennis had an understanding of mixed status in which being Black/White mixed race was seen as being part of a distinct race (and collective experience) in its own right, and one that provides a sense of continuity and community for children, whose own parents are also mixed. These participants very much embraced their Black heritage, and to call themselves and their children "mixed" was not a means of distancing themselves from their Black ancestry, as has been suggested by some analysts in the United States. If anything, their cases suggest the emergence of a mixed Black/White multiracial identity, especially where kinship between monoracial Black people and partially Black people is relatively common and widespread in particular metropolitan areas.[16] By comparison, we did not find such a collective identification as mixed among our other mixed participants (though direct comparisons were made difficult by the fact that there were many more Black/White participants than other types of mixed people in this study). Arguably, a union of two multiracial people of the same background (such as the way Gemma described a "double-mix" union) may be very different from a relationship between two multiracial individuals who share no ethnic or racial ancestry.

Therefore, the identification of children as "mixed" did not necessarily mean the same thing for different participants. While those with minority, White, or multiracial partners could have both different and similar concerns regarding the racial identifications of their children, what it meant to choose "mixed" could be motivated by a variety of factors, including a principled insistence on recognizing all of their children's racial ancestries (regardless of their physical appearance); the desire to assert the emergence of a collective, mixed family experience that was somehow distinctive (or in the case of some Black/White mixed people, their membership in a community of Black/White mixed people); and for those with White partners, a wish to maintain an intergenerational link with a minority heritage, as they faced concerns about racial dilution.

Those Who Chose White

In comparison with the 40 participants who identified their children as multiracial, 14 of 62 parents reported that they classified their children as White. And while these respondents tended to explain their choices in quite similar ways, each account was inflected with the particularities of their own personal histories and experiences. Just as a "mixed" identification for children did not mean the same things, so too with "White," and so it is imperative that we unpack what is meant by "White" in these parents' designations.[17] Of these 14, 7 South Asian/White (of a total of 19), 4 Black/White (of a total of 32), and 3 East Asian/White (of a total of 11) parents designated their children as White. *All* of these 14 parents had White British partners, with the exception of one, whose partner was White German. Other than in this one case, those with non–British White partners did not tend to choose "White," so that their partner's foreign country of birth or ethnicity seemed to disrupt a dominant and mainstream understanding of Whiteness as being White British.

A number of the parents who identified their children as White expressed uncertainty about how to identify them. For instance, Khalil (South Asian/White, 62) talked about why he would choose "White British" for his children:

> I guess I do see them as having a mixed heritage, but it's not something I have emphasized to them and it won't have come through overtly to them through their childhood. My parents died before they were born, and, although they have met a few family members on my father's [Indian] side, and both have been to the Indian subcontinent, I haven't done a very good job in making my side of the family real to them.

Later, he added:

> I guess I would tick the "White British" box, but it wouldn't be a straightforward decision . . . it's simply uncertainty! How many generations does

it take for the mix in parental backgrounds to become so diluted that it is no longer significant?

Khalil and his English wife had not made a point of emphasizing his Indian heritage, and he had not had a particularly Indian upbringing by his father. Furthermore, his observation about generational remove and whether generational distance from a minority heritage eventually renders that heritage essentially insignificant due to "dilution" informed his understanding of (and rationale for) why "White British" was the most appropriate box for his daughters. While Khalil regarded himself as a "mixed" person (and did not look unambiguously White to others), he had been raised as British, and as such, he equated Whiteness with an absence of definable ethnic or racial characteristics[18] and/or an absence of feeling ethnically or racially different from others.[19]

Rose (East Asian/White, 45) articulated some similar sentiments. When asked how she would identify her children on forms, Rose indicated that she would usually choose "White":

Well, it's interesting because I often just don't . . . I just say, "Oh, they're White," and I just leave it at that. . . . And it's partly that I just can't be bothered. I just think well what would be the point? So I . . . just think, well . . . it's like rounding numbers up.

This "rounding up" numbers remark is clearly meant as a metaphor for the dominant proportion of White racial ancestry "in" her children. In addition to the fact that Rose felt that she had been raised with little exposure to her Chinese background (and was in this way similar to Khalil), she reported that her children looked wholly White to her and to others. She recalled how her son, at one point, had described himself to others:

My 10-year-old is very aware of this [his Chinese ancestry] and he went through a phase of going around telling everybody that he's Chinese: "I'm Chinese," and we're all thinking, "What? What are you talking about?"

Here, Rose appeared to be concerned about the possibility of others ridiculing this claim, given that her son reportedly had wholly White features. But in addition, Rose seemed uncomfortable with the idea of her son claiming to be Chinese when he had very little understanding of what that could mean in terms of lived experiences. By saying, "Oh, they're White," Rose skirts the need to explain and justify an assertion that her children are mixed or partly Chinese. Rose discerned that others would not legitimate the idea that her children were "really" Chinese, and thus avoided such scenarios by simplifying their identification as White. For Rose, "White" signified not only her children's embodiment as European-looking, but also their lack of Chinese attributes (other than a bloodline that is not visible to others).

Although Rose identified her children as "White," she and a number of other parents indicated that they did not always take official forms very seriously ("I just can't be bothered"), and could even fill them in variably, as it suited them. However, Rose reported that she was likely to take racial categorization more seriously if it was a medical form and that she might put down "mixed." For her, it all depended on "how much energy [she has] got," and what she thought the form was for.

In addition to the South Asian/White and East Asian/White participants who identified their children as White, four Black/White participants also did so: however, two of these four parents were second-generation mixed (that is, these participants had a parent who was Black/White mixed), and it was clear that this additional generational remove was significant in their deliberations. Glen (Black/White, second-generation, 41) was very clear that while he had some Black ancestry on his mother's side, this had very little meaning for him or his children. For this respondent, generational distance was significant in his explanation for why he did not see himself or his children as multiracial:

> But personally I would only consider somebody that I have met to be mixed race if they are first generation really. . . . So my mother is mixed race, but I'm not.

Because Glen did not consider himself to be mixed race, the notion that his children, another generation down—third generation, could be multiracial, or even part Black, seemed virtually nonsensical to him. According to Glen, his children looked White and their wider social network was mostly White. Glen had had very little contact with his multiracial mother, as she left their home during his childhood, when his parents divorced. As a result, Glen had grown up with his White British father and White British stepmother and with a lot of exposure to his father's White side of the family. Not surprisingly, Glen's case illustrates that the upbringing and experiences of the multiracial parent can strongly influence the way in which the parent identifies his or her own children. A parent who does not value being multiracial or particularly identify as multiracial (or as having a minority ancestry), is unlikely to identify his or her own children as such.

In contrast to Glen, Anna, another second-generation Black/White participant (aged 44), reported that while *she* identified herself as mixed, she didn't do so for her children:

> Yeah. I don't . . . I mean I don't know where you draw the line and when I was younger I used to wonder whether I should or whether I shouldn't [identify as mixed] and . . . and then I decided that I should because I felt like it had influenced my life and who I am and I had felt part of a mixed-heritage, mixed-race family as a child that had been quite clear to me. . . . I'm an eighth Caribbean and that feels like a kind of . . . no, a quarter, sorry. A quarter Caribbean and that feels like a kind of significant kind of percentage of who you are. That's a bit of a kind of crude way of putting it but it felt like it's . . . it's significant but with the kids it felt like it was just too removed. They weren't actually living with a parent who anybody else might identify [as non-White, as Anna was usually seen as White] even so it felt like it would be stretching it.

Interestingly, while Glen, who was second-generation mixed (like Anna), believed that being the child of a multiracial parent did not make him "mixed race," Anna *did* identify as mixed, because she (unlike Glen) had been immersed in both a nuclear and extended family in which she was in contact with family members who were Black or partially Black. And her family had grown up in a semirural setting in England where they were one of the only non-White families; thus her childhood and adolescence had been marked by her awareness of her family's racial difference from most others in her locality.

Clearly, for Anna, the fact that her children's Black Caribbean heritage was even more distant meant that to identify them as mixed was "stretching it"; they were just too far removed from the generational locus of Black heritage. Had her children looked more racially ambiguous to others (they had very fair complexions, blonde hair, and blue eyes), this may have swayed Anna to identify them as mixed. But her children had no lived experience of being partly Black Caribbean.

Kevin (South Asian/White, 39) expressed a similar view about his two young children:

> From my point of view, I'd normally categorize them as being White British, and the reason I do that is I try and work out the proportion of all the ingredients. . . . My mum is Scottish and then with my wife being wholly Scottish, I see that the Asian side of the family is pretty diluted; it was pretty diluted with me. So by the time it gets to the boys, it's even further diluted if you like.

Here, Kevin echoes Anna's reference to blood quantum by referring to how "diluted" (out of "all the ingredients") his Asian heritage is in his children. Some parents, like Matt (South Asian/White, 50), eschewed what they regarded as the mechanistic and "tiresome" logic of racial fractions. Accordingly, Matt saw his son (who was fair and ginger) as "just British"—a sentiment which is reminiscent of Rose's remark about "rounding up" above.

> Well, we joke, we say, "Now Taylor, you're a quarter this, and an eighth that," but really, at the end of the day I find that quite tiresome. And I

wouldn't. I don't think I would. I don't know if we've had to do that. I think he's just British. I think he's just White British I suppose.

In all of these excerpts, it is clear that children's physical appearance as White was fundamental (though it did not necessarily determine) to how participants categorized their children on forms. These parents understood that, despite their actual mixed ancestry, they lived their day-to-day lives as White people—and that this was the way in which they were seen by others. Thus the combination of a White (British) partner, the White physical appearance of children, and in many cases an upbringing in which the parent's own minority heritage had not been stressed (which could engender anxieties about ethnic and racial authenticity), along with generational remove (which was even more pronounced for second-generation mixed parents), was significant in shaping these parents' identification of their children as White.

Those Who Refused to Classify Their Children

While only 5 participants reported that they refused to tick boxes on official forms, as a point of principle, many of the participants who had been willing to identify their children racially also expressed skepticism or dissatisfaction with the classification schemes they encountered in their daily lives. For example, Malcolm (26), who was second-generation mixed (Black/White), did not fill in forms on behalf of his young son, and said: "Them [sic] forms . . . I don't believe in those statistics, and I don't pay any attention to those forms. . . . And people never know how I fit in, since my dad was part Ghanian and my mother English and French." Malcolm believed that forms of racial categorization and statistics were of questionable value and validity, and his own generational remove from his minority ancestor on his father's side (his father was mixed race) contributed to his sense of uncertainty and skepticism about racial classification schemes, and how they might be employed.

Evelyn (South Asian/White, 43) refused to classify her children, and she was strongly opposed to labels being applied to them. This was because she wanted her children to be "independent" of dominant categorizations and labels, and to be "mentally free," not "caged" in by official classifications, which either stereotyped or racially excluded her children.

> I feel other people put you in boxes to take your freedom away, not intentionally, but that's what it ultimately does—it cages you in your own mind and I don't . . . I have liberated myself or have always been like that and I think that's a lot to do with my mother and I will do the same for them [her children]. I don't want them to be caged by other people's perceptions.

Some parents who acknowledged that they were mixed and were even willing to identify their children as "mixed" on forms still rejected or questioned the idea and ontology of race and racial difference. For instance, Joe (Black/White, 49), who normally chose "mixed" to describe his children, was uncomfortable with the idea of race and racial difference and refuted the salience of race for who he was, and by extension, who his children were. Rather than identifying racially, as such, he reported that he felt culturally very English.

> I think I've always felt English in some sort of core way and it's probably because I've a very close identification with my [White English] mother. . . . And all these . . . all these other things about skin tone and all that other stuff, it's kind of . . . it is part of who I am but it's . . . I suppose I don't really feel that. . . . I'd quite like to reject race all together actually—I think that's what it comes down to. . . . For example, when people talk about being proud of being black, I . . . I struggle with that idea. I just . . . I struggle with the idea that it's something to be proud of. It's like . . . to me, it feels very equivalent. It feels equivalent to the idea that someone would say, "I'm proud to be White," and . . . in a racist society—which I think Britain is—kind of white pride sounds, you know . . .

So while Joe understood the political and historical contexts in which Black pride movements and discourses emerged, he could not relate to ethnic and racial pride and politics which somehow privileged his racial self; ultimately, the label "Black" or "mixed" did not capture who he was as an individual.

Discussion and Conclusion

By focusing upon parents who are multiracial themselves, this chapter extends existing research in the United States on how parents in interracial unions classify their multiracial children and illuminates the motivations and meanings underlying the choices made by them. It also provides insight into how participants' own upbringings, the racial ancestry of partners, the physical appearance of children, and the generational locus of mixture can influence parents' racial designations of their children.

The cases discussed in this chapter demonstrate the significant limitations of relying solely on census data for interpreting the choices that parents make. Census tick boxes cannot tell us anything about how or why children are identified in particular ways or reveal any potential uncertainty or ambivalence underlying such choices. Given the lack of clear conventions about identifying second-generation mixed people, these parents' racial designations are best understood as a reflection of how they see (and/or want to see) their children. For many multiracial parents, identifying their own children was far from straightforward, and it was evident that many had reflected considerably on this issue. However, not all participants regarded official forms very seriously, and some refuted their legitimacy. Furthermore, some parents could identify their children variously, depending on context and purpose; for instance medical forms requesting ethnic information could be treated differently from other forms.[20]

The majority of participants (40 of 62) in this study identified their children as "mixed," while only 14 identified their children as White or

White British. Interestingly, *none* identified their children in relation to a non-White single race, such as Black or Asian, even in cases where there was a shared minority race between the parents. The fact that so many of our multiracial participants identified their own children as mixed suggests that *a sense of generational continuity in multiracial identification was important for many participants.* Overall, this propensity to identify their children as mixed also suggests that many of our respondents were committed to *the idea* of recognizing their children as multiracial.

For many parents, choosing "mixed" was a principled assertion of the importance of recognizing *all* of their children's racial ancestries and about emphasizing family relatedness and continuity (as multiracial), regardless of children's appearance, blood quantum, or generational remove from minority ancestry. Even the small number of participants with partners with whom they shared a minority ancestry felt compelled to choose "mixed," so that they did not deny their children's White heritage (however small). For those with White partners, choosing "mixed" was an emotive assertion of not being "just White," as they were insisting upon their children's link with a minority heritage that was generationally more tenuous than it was for themselves.

By comparison, the minority of parents who identified their children as *White* tended to explain their choices in terms of the physical appearance of their children as wholly White, the generational locus of "mixture" as being too far removed to have any real meaning or relevance for their children (especially in the case of second-generation mixed parents), and/or a lack of a feeling of belonging in or knowledge of their minority ancestry and culture. Some of these parents also believed that a White identification for their children was the only one that would be validated by others, given their children's White appearance.

As we have seen, then, the choice of specific terms such as "mixed" or "White" does not speak for itself but requires further scrutiny. For instance, while some parents used "White" to convey their children's corporeal Whiteness, others used "White" as a shorthand for "British," which meant "White" referred to their primary sense of belonging in

Britain (as opposed to some other place and culture) and/or to their lack of cultural competence in or sense of belonging to the country from where a non-British ancestor originated. In this sense, "White" often conveyed the default mode, culturally, for these children, in the case of parents who themselves had little connection with their minority "roots."[21]

Although some participants (with White partners) who had children who looked wholly White to others still opted to assert a "mixed" identification for their children, it is notable that no parents (especially Black/White participants) with children with a non-White or racially ambiguous appearance felt able to claim a White identification for their children (though none of the parents explicitly reported that they wished to do so when their children were not seen as White by others). In this way, we can distinguish between participants who feared that the assertion of a mixed identity for their children may be ridiculed (if, for example, a child looked White to others) from those participants (especially those with Black ancestry) who understood that to claim a White identification on behalf of their children was not just an invitation to ridicule, but was itself a historically laden form of racial rejection. The few Black/White participants who did identify their children as White did so because with generational distance and a wholly White appearance on the part of their children, a White identification would not be challenged. So while many parents in this study recognized some degree of options in how they identified their children, especially in settings and situations that were marked by ethnic and racial diversity, they were by no means unconstrained in how they felt able to exercise those options.

So, how influential was a partner's ancestry for the identification of children? In the cases where there was a shared minority race between the couple, this did *not* result in the participant identifying their child in relation to that shared minority heritage on official forms. Instead, all of those children were identified as multiracial. Many of our respondents had a *shared overlap of Whiteness* with their partners since all of our respondents were part White and most (46 of 62) participants had White partners. Yet most of such households (32 of 46) still classified their children as "mixed." While many parents said that all of their children's heritages were important, they also observed that they did not need to highlight their children's White heritage (unless it was specifically non-British, such as German, or Polish, or Irish, and so on) since Whiteness was all around them (especially for those who lived in more suburban settings in the South East). In most cases, it was understood that no particular effort had to be made in relation to explicitly valuing or identifying (British) Whiteness. While the sample is too small to identify a clear pattern, those with White "other" (non-British) partners, especially if they were ethnically distinct in terms of language (such as Italian or German) and raised in another country, seemed less inclined to choose "White" than those who had White British partners. It may be that those with non-British White partners chose "mixed" in part to assert the ethnic and cultural distinctiveness of the non-British partner.

Thus, having a White partner or having a monoracial minority partner with whom there was racial overlap did not guarantee that children would be identified in relation to that shared race as White or as non-White. Just as Bratter found that in the United States a shared Black heritage did not guarantee that couples would identify their child as Black (though such couples were more likely to classify their children as Black than multiracial),[22] this British study found that a shared minority ancestry with a partner (including a shared Black ancestry) did not result in the identification of children in a monoracial minority category. Thus spousal ethnicity and the physical appearance of children, along with other key factors such as generational distance/remove, *shaped, but did not determine* the ways in which parents identified their children. Because we did not interview the partners of our participants (with the exception of one partner who was present during the interview, above), we do not know the degree to which they would agree with how our participants identified their children, but it would not be surprising if there were some differences between parents in some of these households.

Despite the choices that these parents made, the filling in of an official form is a private act and one that is not subject to scrutiny or challenge on the basis of one's appearance or lifestyle in social interactions. In prior studies in the United States, the racial identifications of children tended to be regarded as a proxy for how parents socialize their children, so that if a Black and White couple designated their child as "Black," it was taken to imply that such a child was raised as Black. Yet without studies demonstrating that there is such a link between the identification and upbringing of children (parenting practices), this remains only an educated guess. Moreover, we cannot readily assume that the ways in which multiracial parents racially identify their children corresponds neatly with the ways in which they raise their children in their day-to-day lives. That is the focus of the next chapter.

3

The Parenting Practices of Multiracial People

This chapter explores the ways in which mixed people in Britain think about their parenting and the practices they employ in raising their children. What approaches and practices do multiracial parents in contemporary Britain adopt in relation to their children? To what extent is it important for these parents to raise their children with an awareness of their minority ancestries? How do the participants' own identifications and life experiences (including how they themselves were raised) shape the ways in which they wish to raise their children?

The *upbringing* of multiracial children—which is related to, but not synonymous with, the racial identification of multiracial children—is still under-studied. Nor are parenting practices easily captured or investigated in analyses of large data sets. We know very little about the particular concerns of multiracial individuals who are parents (as compared to interracial couples with first-generation multiracial children) or whether multiracial people want to steer their children toward a particular kind of upbringing.

Unsurprisingly, there is widespread agreement that parents play a fundamental role in shaping their children's sense of selves vis-à-vis others and the wider society. Much of the literature on multiracial families concerns how parents can foster the healthy development of multiracial children.[1] As one influential book called *Raising Biracial Children* strongly argues: "Because of the power of race, parents raising mixed-race children have a responsibility to engage in a process of racial socialization that will prepare their children to understand and effectively negotiate the complexities of race relations."[2] Yet some Black and White parents in interracial unions (and by extension, couples in other types of interracial unions) may adopt a "color blind" racial ideology, which minimizes the importance of race and its significance.[3]

Parents' awareness and understanding of racial issues, and their willingness to discuss and to validate their multiracial children's perspectives and experiences, are said to be crucial for the development of healthy identities.[4] In a recent Pew survey of multiracial Americans, participants reported talking with their children about their racial backgrounds "sometimes" or "often," and certainly more than their own parents had—a finding that suggests a generational shift in parenting culture and racial awareness.[5]

According to Ravinder Barn, "The process of socialization entails the acquisition of culturally relevant norms and values leading to successful adjustment and personal and social competence in children. This is said to occur through contextual learning via roles and in interaction with others. A key assumption is that parents play a crucial role in the racial and cultural competence of children."[6] Thus, children grow up in a specific "racial environment," which is shaped by particular norms and practices.[7] In Britain, some recent studies of White mothers of children with Black ancestry have shown that they can actively work at teaching and socializing their children to take pride in their Black heritage—thereby countering the mainstream view that has questioned their competence to raise their children with racial awareness or to foster their children's sense of belonging in the wider Black "community."[8] In fact, Winddance Twine argues that White mothers can work hard at developing what she calls "racial literacy" in order to raise their children with both practical knowledge and coping strategies in relation to racist encounters.[9] She also found that some White mothers provided forms of supplementary education about Black history and cultural practices and learned to adopt a "black signature" via the cooking of Caribbean food and caring for their children's hair. Some studies of transracial adoption have also explored the concerns and practices related to the socialization of adopted children. Clearly, parents' conceptualizations of race and ethnicity, as well as their racial ideologies, are critical in shaping the racial socialization of their children.[10]

Nevertheless, given the variable experiences and perspectives of disparate kinds of mixed people and their families, there is no one template that can be applied to how parents of mixed children raise or should raise them. In a discussion of race matching in adoption and fostering policies, Chamion Caballero and her colleagues convincingly argue that, given the great diversity of experiences for children in families of mixed ethnic and racial backgrounds, there cannot be "a single benchmark" of how to raise such children; thus, a rigid application of an ethnic or racial matching policy may be misguided.[11] By the same token, we can expect multiracial people who are parents to think about and practice their parenting in quite disparate ways.

Clearly, various types of parent-child interactions can shape a child's sense of self and well-being. Both the quantity (the amount of time parents spend with children in particular activities and contexts) and quality of parental involvement (based upon the degree of emotional closeness and communication between parents and their children) affect parents' socialization of their children.[12] And while the influence of peers grows as children grow older, there is no doubt that parents play an absolutely fundamental role in their children's upbringing, whether through acts of commission or omission.

Parenting Approaches and Practices

The parents in this study were asked about how they raised their children and about the relative importance of imparting an awareness of their minority ancestries to them. In the process, these participants were probed about both their beliefs and practices regarding the upbringing of their children, and they were also asked to reflect upon their own upbringing and formative life experiences.

In referring to the upbringing of children, I mean a variety of practices, including modes of identity transmission (such as telling the child that he or she is Zimbabwean or mixed race or giving the child an identifiably ethnic name); ways of engendering a sense of cultural attachment (for example, by targeted activities such as museum visits or speaking another language); and efforts to talk with them about recognizing and coping with forms of racial prejudice and discrimination. Such practices are also part of a wider set of family practices, or what David Morgan calls "fragments of daily life which are part of the normal taken-for-granted existence by its practitioners."[13] While some parents in the study gravitated toward a discussion of ethnic and cultural transmission, others spoke more of how they fostered racial awareness and pride. Some parents also articulated concerns about cultural and ethnic loss. A small number of parents reported that they made no concerted effort to foster ethnic and racial attachments or identification or to promote racial awareness. While there were no discernible gender differences in how male and female participants *thought and talked about* how to raise their children, in practice, the mothers (including the female partners of our male participants) tended to adopt a more active role in their children's upbringing, as they were more often the main caregivers of young children.

As revealed in the accounts below, a number of factors were important in shaping the ways in which parents raised their children, including their locality, the ethnicity of their partner or ex-partner(s), the presence or absence of the other parent while their children were growing up, the physical appearance of their children, their upbringing by *their* parents (and the quality of those relationships), and crucially, their own racial identifications and experiences more generally. It was not uncommon, for instance, for some participants to speak ruefully about how they had been raised by their own parents. Alan (South Asian/White, 53) spoke passionately about the difficulties he experienced growing up and how his Bengali father's lack of communication about his ethnic background or his wider family in Bangladesh was unthinkable to him now:

> So . . . the effect it had on me [negative racial interactions] was that people were treating me in that certain way but I had absolutely nothing to

hang it on . . . especially if you've been given no family members. . . . And all I heard was the occasional very loud, blurted out Bengali conversation on the phone at Christmas. So [he] didn't give me the language, didn't tell me his family names, he's one of eleven. Never met my grandparents. He didn't go for 20 years. Sending money back, but didn't go. So he had it in a little pocket, just inside his skin. And it wasn't going to be shared with anyone. So it wasn't much use to me, I would have liked to have known all that stuff, and then if people were saying all sorts of things about me I could have actually said, "Well, stuff you, I know who I am." So that affected my parenting in a pretty dramatic, very profound way.

Alan was determined not to replicate his own upbringing with his children, and this meant regular and open discussions about his and his wife's ancestries and family histories.

Although explicit discussions with especially young children about race or prejudice were relatively rare, parents who lived in predominantly White areas outside of metropolitan centers could be especially vigilant about their children's reactions to others and how they appeared to be learning or thinking about race and difference, often through the signifier of skin color. They then were able to use their children's comments or observations about others' physical appearance to start discussions with their children and diffuse negative conceptions of difference or any brewing wariness (on the part of their children) with regard to non-White "others." So while some parents consciously addressed particular concerns about race or identity, others wanted to (in the words of one parent) "keep things simple," especially in the case of younger children.

Some of the parents in the study expressed uncertainty or ambivalence about how to prepare their children for their interactions with others as they grew up. Tanya (Black/White, 34) had three sons between the ages of one and seven with her White British husband:

Whether it's [forms of racial prejudice and stereotyping] going to be less for them, it's a tricky one to know what to arm them with and what to give to them, and what to allow them to come to by themselves, because you don't want to burden them, and it's a tricky one. Or do you equip them? Because I wasn't equipped, my [white] mother didn't equip me, really. So I don't know. I think it would be pretty weird if I sat them down and said, "Listen, you are black and that's all you need to know." Like, I don't think that's how they're going to self-identify.

The accounts in this chapter reveal parenting to be an on-going process. As children grew older, parents were able to interact with them in ways that acknowledged the individual personalities and proclivities of their children. After a comprehensive review of all 62 interview transcripts (with missing/incomplete data in three cases), four main modes of bringing up children were identified:

• Raising children as British (8)
• Raising children as mostly British with ethnic symbolism (9)
• Raising children with an emphasis on minority heritage (8)
• Raising children with an emphasis on cosmopolitanism (34)

While there are always some cases which are ambiguous or may appear to fit more than one category, the coding typology was specific enough to allow us to place each case into a category that captured the main mode of upbringing reported by each participant. Of the 62 respondents, not only did just over half of them report an emphasis on cosmopolitanism; a cosmopolitan emphasis was also *the most common among each of the 3 types of mixed respondents*: 18 (of 32) Black/White, 10 (of 19) South Asian/White, and 6 (of 11) East Asian/White. The three other modes were less common.

So, what correspondence was there between how the multiracial participants in this study racially identified their children with how they raised them in their day-to-day lives? In the last chapter, I reported that 40 of 62 participants identified their children as "mixed," 14 participants identified their children as White, 5 refused to identify their children, and 3 did not know or could not say. Interestingly, none identified their children in terms of a "single race" minority race. Many of the 40 participants who identified their children as "mixed" in the last chapter reported parenting practices that were "cosmopolitan," although a small number reported raising their children with an emphasis on their minority heritage, and an even smaller number said they raised their children as "mostly British," or "British." Only half the participants (7 of 14) who *identified* their children as White also reported raising them as British; instead, many of those who identified their children as "White" raised them with an emphasis on cosmopolitanism. So as will be discussed below, the ways in which parents could identify their children on official forms did not necessarily correspond neatly with a specific mode of upbringing or parenting practices.

Raising Children as British

In our sample of 62 parents, 8 participants reported that they raised their children as British. With the exception of one participant (who identified her children as "mixed"), 7 of these 8 participants had identified their children as White. By "British," these participants meant that their children were raised without any specific ethnic emphasis. For most of these participants, Britishness was understood in terms of norms and practices associated with a primarily White mainstream (though one that was increasingly inflected with diversity).

In a small number of cases, participants who raised their children as British did so in part as a negative reaction against their minority ancestries. For instance, Alberto (South Asian/White, 39) identified his young daughter as "White European" and was raising her as an "ordinary British kid." Alberto explained that his daughter's mother was White British, but more significantly, he himself reported being much more "European" than Pakistani (his father's ethnicity) and expressed a number of negative views about what he saw as Asian Muslim cultural practices and politics. Related to these views, Alberto wanted to ensure that his daughter was not in any way stigmatized by being seen as anything other than a White European: "I wanted her to be raised as a European kid. I didn't want her to have to go through any kind of crap or any kind of, you know racial tension." In another case, Jane (East Asian/White, 47) provided an unabashedly negative assessment of her Vietnamese heritage. She had very little contact with her Vietnamese father growing up and had been raised primarily by her British mother and British stepfather. Not only did Jane identify her children as "British," but she was adamant about instilling what she considered to be British values, which she saw as less traditional, and more progressive (though she was not naively positive about Britain): "I have experienced Vietnamese . . . well Vietnamese immigrant culture as it exists in [X], and I don't find it at all attractive and it's not something that I'd want my children to . . . have anything . . . I find it very traditional. It is unbelievably oppressive for women."

In comparison with Alberto and Jane, most of the parents who raised their children as British did not feel negatively about their minority ancestries. Instead, they reported that their minority heritage was either not particularly important to them or of very little relevance to their daily lives. A key theme here was the distance they felt from their ethnic ancestry, which was heightened by additional genealogical distancing in the case of some (though not all) second-generation mixed participants. Generally speaking, these parents did not engage in practices that highlighted an ethnic ancestry or identity other than Britishness, and they reported that their own parents had not raised them with any other ethnic emphasis or repertoire. Additionally, some participants had not been raised with their minority parent, so that their exposure to any other cultural background had been either nil or extremely limited.

For instance, when asked about how she and her White British husband raised their son, Aisha (South Asian/White, 50), who had identified her son as "British," said that she and her husband also raised him as British and that she had made no effort to play up the fact of her Indian father's heritage. Aisha had grown up with her British mother, after her parents had split up when she was extremely young. Consequently, she'd had no meaningful contact with her father and felt no sense of connection to Indian people or heritage.

Aisha also reported that her 13-year-old son had not shown much curiosity about her father or her Indian background, so the fact of her South Asian background just didn't arise for her and her family. As she put it, "there's no concealment, not wanting to talk about it."

> Equally I don't know a lot to tell him, so it's . . . and I don't know whether that might change. I don't think so, I've never had particularly an urge whereas a lot of people like [a close friend] say, "Oh how interesting, how fascinating, you must want to find out more? Or you must want to go there [India]?" Well, no, not really.

Aisha often encountered others' expectations that her Indian background was somehow significant to her—even though it wasn't. Such expectations were compounded by the fact that she looked completely "Asian" to others (and had an identifiably Asian name). This racial assignment of her clearly irritated Aisha at times, as she simply did not see herself as such. Nevertheless, although she saw herself and her son as British, Aisha regarded herself as someone who was very interested in pursuing a pervasive multicultural milieu in her city and social networks. For example, many of her friends were "international" (her words), and she reported that she enjoyed living in a relatively ethnically diverse setting. So, interestingly, her identification of her son as British seemed to be more about an implicit disavowal of her Indian ancestry than a distancing from people and cultures that were not British—as evidenced in her friendships with many non-British people.

For those participants who grew up in almost entirely White settings, an emphasis on a British upbringing was understood as a "natural" outcome, rather than a deliberate fostering of White Britishness, per se. In other words, it was effectively the default mode of childrearing. Elise

(Black/White, 44), who was not partnered at the time of interview, lived in a very small and White village in the South East with her five children (ranging in age between seven and twenty-six)—though the eldest no longer lived at home. Interestingly, Elise had *identified* all of her children as "mixed" (because she believed that was the most appropriate category for them), but in terms of her parenting and family life, she reported that she felt very British and that her children were raised in this way. In fact, Elise spoke of the fact that while others always saw her as monoracially Black, she did not feel Black. As she sheepishly reported, "But to actually know me, then . . . then that's, you know, I could . . . I've always sort of thought my sort of identity is more White really." Because her parents separated when she was very young, she had grown up with little contact with her Black Caribbean father. Reflecting upon her lack of exposure to him, Elise said:

> I've been thinking about this, about my father, and I've talked to my brother about it actually. My father's quite . . . quite White in his attitudes as well. So, I don't think we probably would have had that much of a different upbringing, I don't think.

Elise had lived only in White semirural settings, and all of her partners had been White British. Like Aisha, Elise had no cultural exposure to her Black heritage growing up and felt, at most, a sense of "curiosity," but not one that had motivated her to delve further:

> Erm . . . (pause) I've never really felt that it was important. But as I've got older, and I think it's more of a curiosity I think, it's just a curiosity of knowing where your ancestry is and that's more really, it's just curiosity, it's not, it's not important in terms of that's what I feel that I should be teaching my children, that type of thing. We should [not] adopt, sort of like, a Black culture or anything like that. I, you know, it's just of more for me personally it's more a curiosity really.

Nevertheless, while Elise did not emphasize any ethnic and cultural heritage other than British in her children's upbringing, she still noted the importance of instilling racial awareness in her children, especially because she and some of her children looked "Black" to others. Elise's case demonstrates the importance of looking beyond the chosen identifications of parents in surveys, because her identification of her children as "mixed" did not capture her complex feelings about identifying primarily as a White British person, while also realizing that both she and her children could be subject to prejudice and forms of racial stereotyping in their home, school, and work lives.

Our Black/White participants were particularly attuned to the gendered ways in which their sons or daughters could be racialized by others. Researchers in the United States and Britain have found that multiracial women tended to have their mixed ancestries recognized more easily than multiracial men, who were more likely to be seen as monoracial minorities and subject to stereotypes about criminality.[14] In fact, some parents who were raising boys and young men who might be perceived as Black—due either to visible signifiers such as skin color and hair type, or to their sociocultural performances of "black culture" (through music, rap, style of clothing and/or walking), or to their being attached to groups of Black boys or "gang-culture"—expressed their concerns about preparing their sons for the possibility of being viewed in negative and stereotypical ways. Similarly, the parents of girls often spoke of the need to be extra vigilant about their daughters' perceptions of themselves and their developing conceptions of beauty.

Thus, those who reported raising their children as British were less attached to their ethnic minority backgrounds and made no concerted efforts to expose their children to their minority heritage via discussions or targeted activities. Nevertheless, many of these participants still tended to value and participate in low-level forms of multicultural engagement endemic in the wider society. For instance, cooking and eating ethnic foods, attending ethnically inflected events, or having friends of different ethnic backgrounds was not particularly unusual, and increasingly constituted parts of normal mainstream family life in Britain. Furthermore, raising their children as culturally British did not preclude parenting practices that encouraged forms of racial awareness.

Raising Children as Mostly British but with Symbolic Ethnicity

The 9 participants in this category reported that while they raised their children primarily as British, it was important to retain certain symbolic ethnic and cultural practices and to impart some sense of their minority ancestry to them. While 6 of these 9 participants identified their children as "mixed," 2 identified their children as White, and 1 did not know—thus pointing, again, to the fact that parents' identification of their children does not neatly correspond to a particular mode of upbringing.

What distinguished these participants from those who raised their children as British was their *emotional and symbolic attachment to their minority ethnicity*. While such attachment was not central to their everyday lives, these participants regarded their ethnic backgrounds as personally important. Jeremy, who was South Asian/White (aged 35), had children aged 5 and 8 years old with his White British partner. While he identified his children as "mixed" to reflect his South Asian heritage, their day-to-day lives were mostly British: "Whilst we kind of celebrate the bits and bobs, we're generally quite interested in it all . . . but we're mostly British? That's the world we live in really." Nevertheless, he valued his Indian background, and he reported that it was important that his children developed a sense of this minority heritage as they grew up.

A number of East Asian/White (4) and South Asian/White (3) parents reported raising their children as mostly, but not wholly, British. These parents tended to describe their symbolic ethnic practices in ways that are similar to those of White Americans who engaged in forms of ethnic symbolism and for whom their ethnicities were "optional."[15] However, our participants reported a stronger emotional attachment to their minority backgrounds than in the US studies of Americans with a more distant European heritage.

For example, Beverly (East Asian/White, 43) lived in a mostly White town in the South East with her White British husband and daughters (aged 8 and 10). She had identified her children as "mixed" and reported that her family's day-to-day lives were accented with Chinese food, some Chinese expressions, and the occasional Chinese celebration. For instance, she talked of "little rituals" like giving her children red envelopes that contained money for Chinese New Year or meeting relatives for dim sum in London's Chinatown. So while her attachment to her heritage was symbolically important to her, she was self-conscious about her relatively superficial knowledge of it and felt some anxiety about not being ethnically "authentic."[16]

Concerns about demonstrating ethnic authenticity are not uncommon findings in studies of part Asian mixed people. For example, in her study of Japanese American beauty pageants, Rebecca King-O'Riain found that many of the mixed-race contestants had to work at asserting their racial authenticity through a demonstration of their cultural knowledge of Japanese objects, language, and practices—despite (or because of) their "only" partial Japanese ancestry.[17] Similarly, in this study, various East Asian/White participants articulated the concern that many White people expected them to demonstrate their ethnic and cultural otherness (for instance, by demonstrating fluency in a Chinese dialect or knowing about some aspect of East Asian culture or history). By comparison, Black/White participants were not usually subject to expectations that they demonstrate knowledge of other languages or distinctive cultural practices—although, as illustrated by Elise (above), many Black/White participants spoke of "White" and "Black" ways of being, including behavioral repertoires, in quite essentialist terms.

Some participants who had little knowledge of their East Asian heritage relied upon their parents to provide that cultural link for their own children. Nicole (East Asian/White, 28) identified her infant son as "mixed" and reported that while her knowledge of her Indonesian ancestry was limited, it was still important to her. Nicole lived in a predominantly White suburb in the South, and her Indonesian mother lived nearby. Because she and her White British husband were thinking of moving abroad, she expressed concern that without her Indonesian mother's regular presence, she would be unable to provide her son with a meaningful link to his Indonesian heritage:

> Because I see my mum and I was with her when I was growing up and I know that she's from somewhere else, you know, it sort of all goes in, whereas, with me, you know, I'll always speak to him probably in English, and you know, [her husband] and I will always be conversing in English and there probably won't be that much influence or apparent influence to him that I'm actually Indonesian.

Participants like Nicole expressed a degree of anxiety about the tenuous connection they felt to an ethnic minority heritage and background.[18] Because these respondents tended to have very little language fluency or knowledge of distinctive cultural practices and because they were not part of a wider ethnic social network, it was quite possible that their children would be completely disconnected from that particular ethnic heritage (as in Nicole's case).

As discussed above, the ways in which our multiracial participants identified their children did not necessarily provide a clear picture of how they raised them. Anna (second-generation Black/White, 44), for example, reported on the one hand that she identified her children as White British because she believed that their generational remove from their Black Caribbean ancestry, along with their White appearance, made it difficult (and, she implied, inappropriate) to identify them as "mixed." On the other hand, Anna also reported that her Black/White mother spent a lot of time with her children and that it was important to Anna that they have some appreciation of their Black Caribbean heritage, along with the history of the African diaspora more generally:

> I make sure that I talk to the kids about it [her Caribbean heritage]. I don't . . . I don't talk about something sort of huge and significant that, you

know, it's not like we have any particular events or cultural celebrations or anything like that but they know and we . . . we talk about my mum's heritage and we talk about my granddad and, you know, talk about where he is from and that kind of thing. . . . You know, if you look at my children, it's not an immediate thing that you would think that they had a mixed heritage background in any way, and so I think it could be very easy for it to be totally forgotten and . . . and I didn't want to that to happen.

Anna's identification of her children as "White British," on its own, would not have provided any sense of the strength of ties with her mixed mother or Anna's own political commitment to fostering racial and cultural awareness in her children.

Raising Children with an Emphasis on Minority Heritage

In comparison with the participants discussed above, a small number of participants were very clear that they wanted to raise their children in relation to a specific minority heritage. All but one (who rejected racial categorization and refused to fill in forms) of these 8 participants had identified their children as "mixed." Interestingly, 6 of the 8 respondents who did so were Black/White (6 of 32); only 2 other respondents, both of whom were South Asian/White, reported this emphasis on minority culture. Of these 8 participants, 5 had non-White spouses who were either British or foreign in their upbringing.

These respondents reported that they made a concerted effort to keep their minority heritage/culture alive—though their motivations for doing so differed. For instance, Amanda (47), who was Black/White, made a point of talking with her children (aged 9, 11, and 14) about her father's Black ancestry and "exposing" her children to other Black people. Her children's schools and their neighborhood were primarily White, and in their day-to-day lives, her children were mostly around White people, including her own White British husband—though he was very active in talking with his children about possible forms of racism and introducing them to African music and art. This emphasis on a specific minority heritage could also entail an explicit valuing of minority people and backgrounds more generally, as a counter to the negative portrayals of minority people and cultures they encountered in the media and wider society.

In one case, Dennis (Black/White, 45) had been adopted at a very young age by a White couple in the Midlands. While he thought his parents had been loving and well meaning, they had not been able to provide any link to his Black Caribbean heritage, and this made him determined to impart this heritage to his own children.

> I was brought up in a predominately White area so I was kind of the only Black kid. I didn't really know about mixed race in them days, I was just Black, everybody else was White and I was Black, so . . . it was, yeah it was hard growing up, it was hard growing up. But I looked to these people [his adoptive parents], they'd chosen me regardless of my color so, you know, it was good. . . . [But] there was no cultural fulfilment or anything at all during my childhood. So . . . I just grew up knowing I was different, you know.

As a result of feeling that there had been no "cultural fulfillment" and his experiences of racism growing up, Dennis was clear that he wanted to build a life for himself among Black people, and he reported that he'd consciously had Black or part-Black partners and raised his children as "culturally Black," meaning "Black food, Black TV."[19]

In contrast with Aisha, whose lack of exposure to her minority parent had led her to disregard her Indian heritage, Dennis went in the other direction and reclaimed this "lost" heritage—though their family circumstances (he had been adopted) were not similar. These cases reveal that people who had little exposure to their minority heritage could react quite differently when they became parents themselves and sought to make sense of and to value (or not) a minority background and culture.

Like Dennis, Victor was concerned about revitalizing his Black ancestry in relation to his young son. Victor (second-generation Black/White, 39) was married to a Black African woman. When asked if it was important to pass down his and his wife's Black heritage to his 2-year-old son, he said:

> I think it's very important because . . . like the Sankofa bird . . . it's a bird that comes from Ghana that's called the Sankofa bird. As the bird walks forward he has his head back. He's kind of like an African brother because he never forgets where he came from. And I think it's very important to always remember your past as you go forward. And I'd like to embrace my son in both cultures.

Victor noted that while his Irish background was important to him and he was close to his White Irish mother, he wanted to pass down a Black cultural heritage, especially that of his Black African wife. As a second-generation mixed person, whose own father was (first-generation) mixed, Victor was very fair, and he had to work at asserting his Black heritage. Moreover, Victor reported, with regret, that his father had not raised him with any appreciation of his Black Caribbean ancestry. While Victor identified his son as mixed on official forms, he wanted to ensure that his son developed a pride in his Black ancestry as a bulwark against the racial prejudice that Victor believed he would surely encounter as he grew up. Victor's son was thus given an identifiably African name and was being taught to speak in an African dialect by his mother.

As in the cases of Dennis and Victor, the presence of an ethnic minority and/or foreign spouse could be significant in bringing about an emphasis upon a shared minority heritage. For instance, Laila (South Asian/White, 42) was married to a Bangladeshi man, and they had met in Bangladesh, where she had been working. During her childhood in a White, suburban part of the South East, Laila felt largely denigrated by the White mainstream, and she was clear that she would not have wanted a White British partner, despite being part White herself. While Laila reported that she and her husband did not disregard her White mother's Irish background, they made an effort to teach their daughters (aged 10 and 12) Bengali and to be proud of their Asian ancestry.

However, not all participants had the resources, time, and energy to attend fully to the upbringing and emotional needs of their children, especially if they were single parents who struggled with the day-to-day concerns of survival. This was the case for some working-class participants who had been single parents while raising their children. Tara (Black/White, 50), for instance, reported that she had raised her younger daughter with a strong emphasis upon her Black heritage (her daughter's White father had little contact with her), but that she had not done so in the case of the daughter who was four years older:

> [My older daughter] got very upset and she said to me, . . . "You didn't pass anything on to me." (Laughs ruefully) I was really upset and . . . I thought back and it was true because when [my daughter] was fourteen/fifteen I didn't know anything about myself. . . . I was actually really busy trying to survive being a single parent, you know, with two children and really juggling life, and also I have a very, very difficult family history.

As illustrated above, the themes of cultural and racial loss and revitalization, combined with a conscious effort to counter dominant and negative images and thinking about minority people, informed many of these respondents' ways of thinking about their children's upbringing, especially in the case of people with Black ancestry. The specific attributes of partners, especially if they had not been raised in Britain, could be significant in steering their children's upbringing toward a specific minority heritage. Nevertheless, several participants who raised their children with a minority emphasis had White British or White European partners, who were committed to socializing their children with an appreciation of their minority backgrounds.

Raising Children with an Emphasis on Cosmopolitanism

Just over half of the participants (34 of 62) emphasized a cosmopolitan mode of raising their children. While most (24 of 34) of these participants identified their children as "mixed," a small number (5 of 34) identified them as White, 3 refused to identify their children, and 2 said that they did not know. I use the term "cosmopolitan" to suggest how these parents appreciated ethnic and cultural diversity in contemporary British society, in which many different types of people and hybrid cultural formations are regarded with respect. Furthermore, the participants who articulated this cosmopolitan sensibility also saw themselves and their children as part of an increasingly interconnected global humanity and/or citizenship. These notions echo the theorizing of analysts such as Kwame Anthony Appiah and Elijah Anderson, as well as Paul Gilroy, who writes of "multicultural conviviality" found in contemporary British cities.[20] While a few respondents actually used the term "cosmopolitan," others referred to this concept in other ways, through descriptions of their everyday lives and their various interactions with others.

While these parents valued their children's ethnic backgrounds, in contrast to those who emphasized the importance of passing down a *specific* minority heritage, these participants were more concerned with the idea of their children growing up exposed to a diverse set of people and practices. For instance, Kevin (South Asian/White, 37) believed that a specific focus on his Bangladeshi background was somehow manufactured and forced (and had identified his children as British), but he felt strongly about exposing his children to a cosmopolitan set of experiences:

> We just live in [a London borough] which is great in terms of how multicultural it is, and the boys get on the bus, or they get the train, and you know, there's often a conversation about music or colors or food, or if we walk past a market, of which there are loads, veg and mobile phone

repairs, then I like to pick them up and show them . . . because for me, I think that's a cultural thing.

A number of "cosmopolitan" participants even stated an antipathy to passing down a specific nationality. As Dominique (East Asian/White, 47), a lone parent, put it, "We don't do Chinese, we don't do French, we don't do English" (she had refused to identify her son on forms). While Dominique opposed particular nationalistic attachments, she wanted her son to appreciate a diversity of people, places, and cultural artefacts and practices, and it was still important to her that her 15-year-old son remembered her Chinese father and grandparents and relatives—not because they were Chinese, per se, but because they were family and important to her, just as her French relatives were. In articulating an opposition to a singular nation and nationality, Dominique indicated an appreciation of a more cosmopolitan ethos.

Similarly, Drew (South Asian/White, 47), who had a White British partner, opposed the idea of a strong nationalistic affiliation and identity—and he maintained that he would not know how he would fill in ethnic monitoring forms. In reflecting upon his upbringing by his Indian father and English mother, he noted that his father had not emphasized his Indian heritage:

I mean one of the things I do remember my dad saying once was about, you know, nationality basically being an accident at birth and I think that's kind of colored my perception of the world, that, you know . . . I've always felt primarily that, you know, I'm a human being, if you like, and all the sort of grief and worrying and trouble caused by, you know, national identities is very hard for me to understand because, you know, we grew up in a sort of seamless mix of cultures where, you know, it just wasn't an issue and there was no sort of flag-waving.

As a parent who lived in a mostly White town in the South East, Drew adopted this anti-nationalist, "seamless mix of cultures" view in bringing up his own children (aged 5 and 11), although he also said his visits to India with his children were very important to him, especially in enabling them to remain connected to their Indian relatives. Many of these "cosmopolitan" parents also articulated notions of hope for a post-racial society, where our awareness of ethnic and racial difference would largely recede.

Another parent of two sons (aged 5 and 10), Rose (East Asian/White, 45), who was married to a White British man, had identified her sons as "White," given their appearance and their lack of knowledge of their Chinese heritage. However, in the course of the interview, Rose made it clear that she tried to adopt a cosmopolitan approach in her parenting, and even used the term itself:

> And I don't believe that there's such a thing as a post-racial society but I kind of want him [her older son] to inhabit this sort of post-racial situation . . . and part of that is . . . me saying, "but your, you know, your grandfather was Chinese." Me telling him his grandfather was Chinese has a lot of facets to it and one of them is this sense that I want to bring him up in a . . . in a sort of cosmopolitan . . . kind of frame of mind.

Many of the parents who lived in London observed that their children would experience what Steven Vertovec has called "super-diversity."[21] For some participants, a low-level recognition and enjoyment of *difference* was a way of talking about the mélange of contemporary races, ethnicities, and cultures in London. Thus, as Vanessa (Black/White, 51) said of her children,

> I've actually tried to just incorporate . . . difference in the way I've brought them up so that's why you've got pictures of all different places around the house. And I haven't really forced it down them but I kind of just embraced . . . like we've traveled. I like to travel and go to different places and . . . so I think that's how I've managed it more than to say that, you know, we're [of] any particular background.

In another case, Edward (East Asian/White, 33) and his Black British wife had recently become parents. He lived and worked in an extremely diverse part of London, and stressed both cosmopolitanism *and* the retention of minority culture. Reflecting on his infant son, whom he identified as "mixed," he noted that he wanted to do things differently from his Filipino mother, who had tried to direct him toward Filipino culture when he was growing up.

> Yeah, I think . . . I think he's going to fit right in to where we are now, I
> think in the world. . . . I hope anyway that, you know, he can adapt . . .
> because he's got a very strong Jamaican family and he's got a very strong
> Filipino family and a very strong British family as well and we all identify
> with our British-ness as well. So I think, I think that's going to be great
> for him really anyway, to have that variety is amazing. . . . I just want
> him . . . I think I just want him to be human, really, more than anything.
> I think just to be human and warm and be able to accept different things.
> To be able to celebrate—sounds a bit trite—but to celebrate difference
> is essential and to celebrate change and all of those things are just such
> important things.

In addition to an emphasis on "celebrat[ing] difference," this understanding of cosmopolitanism also emphasized a global humanity that ideally transcended racial and ethnic differences. Thus, this cosmopolitan outlook was one in which some parents valorized and celebrated diversity per se and their children's curiosity for and experience of many different cultures and places, and did not necessarily privilege their *own ethnic* ancestries.

For example, Bina (South Asian/White, 47) lived in London, and had children with her ex-partner, who was also mixed (Japanese/White American). For Bina, "mixed" was the only identification that made sense for her children. Interestingly, Bina spoke of how her daughter (age 23) became immersed in Greek culture, instead of forming an attachment to one of her parents' ancestries:

My sister being in Greece and having a son, their cousin, who's Greek. And they [her children] spent quite a lot of time in Greece doing summer holidays, you know, go and visit her. So Yumiko learnt Greek in fact. . . . And she wanted to become a Greek Orthodox, which kind of like, was like . . . (raises eyebrows and gives surprised face) . . . I didn't really know how to deal with that! (she laughs). It's like . . . ahhh . . .

She continued with this theme later in the interview:

I know, it's a bit weird. . . . It's like . . . if they [children] already didn't have enough on their plate [in terms of their diverse ethnic "mix"], you know? But that's part of who they are, and it's part of where their curiosity leads them. And I'm all for that, I support it totally, I'm not going to say "NO, don't learn Greek, why the hell do you want to learn Greek?!" or "Why don't you learn Japanese instead?" No, I think it's perfectly ok, it's fine, it's good. I mean, I support it totally, it's just about opening up more and learning more.

Clearly, the ethnic and racial composition of where parents lived was important in shaping their socialization of their children. For parents like Edward and Bina, who were raising their children in diverse parts of London, their adoption of cosmopolitan attitudes and practices in their parenting was the norm in their locality and social networks.

Yet, some parents who lived in much less ethnically diverse areas could also make a concerted effort to foster a cosmopolitan outlook with their children. For instance, Jonathon (East Asian/White, 42) had just moved from a relatively cosmopolitan city in Wales to a very White city in the South West with his White British wife and their two sons (5 and 11), and he was concerned to expose his children to a more diverse network of people:

It's really important for them to have a global view of the world. . . . [My wife] gets quite upset about discrimination, thoughtlessness, like thoughtless comments people might make . . . and she worries about it—it's one of her anxieties about living in [city in the South West] actually, is the lack of diversity, whereas in the area that we lived in [before], was a very diverse area, and the school he went to he had lots of Asian friends.

Later, he added:

I see them as Welsh, and I see them mixed race by line, but I'd like to see them as "people of the world," it sounds like a very John Lennon thing to say, but they're Welsh, they're predominantly White, whatever that means, and they have German, Chinese, and Scottish backgrounds, so that's how I'd like to see them.

Jonathon identified his children as "mixed," and in doing so, he put an emphasis on his children being "people of the world," not just mixed in terms of ancestries. Among other things, he saw them as Welsh because they were born in Wales, and not because of any Welsh ancestry. This form of cosmopolitanism stresses the potential for multiple forms of belonging and identification; importantly, it stresses *place* as much as lineage.

In fact, a number of parents made a point of saying that they did not want their children to grow up in a wholly White place. Speaking of their daughter, Claudia (Black/White, 29) said that she and her White husband didn't want her to grow up in a monocultural place:

I don't know whether I felt that more strongly than he did but I wouldn't want . . . Like we talked about moving down to [a sizeable city in the South East] where I used to live . . . and the concerns that I had over that were just that I didn't want her to grow up anywhere too white, for the same reason that I wouldn't want her to grow up anywhere too Black or too Asian. I just wanted her to have . . . to grow up with mixed cultures around her just so that she was aware of different cultures and races from the outset really.

Like Claudia, Matt (South Asian/White, 50) was concerned that moving to a smaller town from London could inhibit his son's development. In spite of the move, though, Matt sees his son now as someone quite open-minded and aware of both his own cultural and ethnic heritage and that of others:

> So Taylor grew up not even questioning it [diversity as a positive thing], and has never had any prejudice in that sense. And . . . his friends, all of them are all mixed race. . . . He may even go abroad. He's got much bigger scope. . . . If he does stay here . . . (he laughs), it will be quite awful. I think it'll be very challenging. Because if he does want to . . . if you like, indulge or look at his cultural identity . . . here is incredibly White, very narrow-minded. . . . I am ever so slightly fearful that he will lose all cultural identity.

Discussion and Conclusion

While this study found four different modes in which participants raised their children—namely, as British; as mostly British but with symbolic ethnicity; with an emphasis on minority heritage; and with an emphasis on cosmopolitanism—these modes are ideal types, and there is clearly some spillage among them. A relatively small number of participants reported raising their children as British, mostly British, or with a minority emphasis, while the majority of participants (of all ethnic "mixes") reported an emphasis upon cosmopolitanism.

A number of factors were clearly important in shaping how our multiracial participants raised their children: the participants' own identifications and upbringings, including their own contact and exposure to their minority parent and their minority relatives and networks; the ethnicity and influence of their partner(s); the physical appearance of their children; and the ethnic diversity (or lack thereof) of their neighborhoods and their children's schools. Some participants who had had little exposure to or little contact with a minority parent and extended family showed little attachment to their minority heritage, and this was also reflected in the fact that they did not cultivate an ethnic attachment for their children. On the other hand, for a few participants a lack of exposure to a minority heritage during their own childhoods galvanized them to revive their minority ancestry, especially in the context of raising their children.

Not surprisingly, both current and former partners could be influential in raising children. Those participants who had a minority partner with whom they shared a minority heritage were more likely to emphasize their shared ancestry in bringing up their children, but the ethnicity of partners did not in itself determine the ways in which our participants engaged in their parenting, just as the ethnicity of partners did not in itself determine the ways in which participants racially *identified* their children (see Chapter 2). Furthermore, having a White British partner did not necessarily correspond to an emphasis on White British socialization, as these White partners could be very invested in raising their children in a more cosmopolitan way or in fostering racial awareness in their children.

While there were no clear-cut differences in how the three types of multiracial participants (Black/White, South Asian/White, East Asian/White) in this study raised their children, it is striking that most of the participants who socialized their children with an emphasis upon a specific minority heritage were Black/White individuals, while none of the East Asian/White participants emphasized a specific East Asian ancestry in their children's upbringing (though those with East Asian ancestry were far fewer in number in this study). In comparison with those Black/White participants who conveyed a strong sense of attachment to and appreciation of their Black ancestries and a wish to convey that heritage to their own children, many of the East Asian/White and South Asian/White participants were much more diffident and tentative about their ethnic and racial ancestries and often expressed anxiety about whether other people, including other "full" Asians, would regard them as being authentically Asian. These findings, which compare part-Asian and part-Black people, chime with those of studies that have compared the racial orientations of Asian Americans and African Americans in the United States. As will be discussed further in the subsequent chapters, in the British context, it may be that those with Black ancestry were, generally speaking, more invested in both societal discourses and family histories that emphasized the importance of asserting Black pride and lineage, while such societal discourses (and publicly visible mobilizations) were less common and/or less recognized in the case of part–East Asian (and part–South Asian) individuals.

In the previous chapter, we learned that most of the parents in this study identified their children as "mixed." However, as I have argued, what "mixed" (or "White") meant required unpacking, and furthermore, as I have illustrated in this chapter, the ways in which parents identified their children did not always correspond neatly with particular modes of parenting. For instance, identifying one's children as "White" on official forms did not preclude the possibility that they were raised with a cosmopolitan emphasis. Furthermore, some participants who had identified their children as "mixed" could, in practice, adopt an emphasis upon a specific minority heritage. Thus parenting practices cannot be straightforwardly "read off" of how participants identify their children. At one level, this is hardly surprising, since people (and their behaviors) are usually far more complex, changeable, and ambivalent than a "tick box" can capture.

Rather than privileging any one ethnic or racial background, the cosmopolitan approach to parenting stressed transcending narrow modes of belonging, in terms of specific ethnic and racial affiliations. For these parents, being multiracial could in itself exemplify this ideal of cosmopolitanism. In large, diverse metropolitan areas, this awareness of ongoing "mixture" was strong.[22] And even parents who reported that they raised their children as "just" British demonstrated ways of parenting strongly influenced by the growing level of multiculturalism present in their daily lives.

Many of our predominantly middle-class sample felt able to take on identities or transcend or redefine them to their needs, even if such efforts were accompanied by some uncertainty or anxiety (since not all such assertions of a particular identity were validated by others). As Peony Faghen-Smith has argued, like other educated middle-class people middle-class multiracial people have a greater sense of entitlement.[23] Nevertheless, some of our working-class participants (such as Victor and Dennis) created the meanings of a mixed Black/White identity and community for themselves and their children.

Interestingly, the ways in which many of the participants in this study (especially those who lived in London and its surroundings) spoke of valuing ethnic and racial diversity in their and their children's lives went beyond what seemed to be superficial appreciations of "diversity." In comparison with Elijah Anderson's discussion of the "cosmopolitan canopy" in a major American city,[24] in which everyday civil interracial interactions did occur, but were finely balanced and quite fragile, in the settings inhabited by many middle-class and educated multiracial individuals in this British study (including many Black/White participants) such "cosmopolitan canopies" were the norm, rather than the exception, and participants were generally quite comfortable in their various social milieus. Somehow, without being naïve about or insensitive to the real injuries of racism, many of these participants articulated a deep embrace of cosmopolitan ideals.

In comparison to how they themselves had been raised, our multiracial participants reported placing a much higher value on ethnic and racial difference in their own parenting practices and everyday family lives. While most of our participants were not themselves raised with a cosmopolitan emphasis, and while their parents did not generally talk with them about racial awareness or pride, this generation of multiracial parents appears to be better equipped to foster multiple ways of belonging for their children.

This study also found a growing normalization of being multiracial and being part of a mixed family.[25] Our findings suggest the importance of avoiding normative conclusions about the "best" way for multiracial individuals (and families) to raise their children.[26] It would be erroneous to conclude that the minority of parents who raised their children with what they believed to be a solely British emphasis are somehow less attentive to their children's multiple needs; as shown in the excerpts above, parents who had relatively little attachment to a minority heritage or parent had no wish to try to manufacture a meaningful minority history or identification for their children if they themselves felt no such connection. Conversely, while the majority of parents in this study reported a cosmopolitan mode of raising their children, such an emphasis on cosmopolitanism should not be automatically assumed to be a healthier or more appropriate approach to parenting children. Despite the rather rose-tinted imagery and language about diversity used by some parents, they were all too aware of how increasing diversity can coexist with continuing tensions and prejudices, as the next chapter will illustrate.

4

Multiracial People, Their Children, and Racism

She hasn't had any problems but I think maybe she's going to start getting to an age where she can see that there is a difference. . . . At pre-school they all made pictures of themselves and in her picture she drew herself as quite brown but I'm not sure whether she did it consciously or whether the teachers told her to do it. . . . All the other children were pink . . . so maybe these kinds of things will start making her think about these things. That's why I'm thinking it will be good to send her to a school with more diversity so that she can also accept herself as well as other people who are different.

—Cecilia (East Asian/White, 31)

As someone who grew up feeling "othered" and devalued on the basis of her racially ambiguous appearance, Cecilia was concerned about how her young daughter was coming to see herself. In the last chapter, we learned of the various ways in which multiracial people brought up their children. Many participants considered it important to prepare their children to navigate the racialized interactions they could encounter as they grew up, and into their adult years. This was especially the case for participants who believed that their children could be racially targeted on the basis of their physical appearance—that is, on the basis of what is often called "observed" race, or how others see someone in racial terms.[1]

Space limitations preclude a fuller discussion, but I use "racism" with the caveat that there is no one accepted conceptualization and understanding of this widely used term; nor can we speak of "racism" as a unitary, monolithic phenomenon.[2] In fact, as I have argued elsewhere, the seemingly ubiquitous references to "racism" in many academic and media writings (and wider popular discourses) have resulted in a worrying lack of precision around its use.[3] Nevertheless, various American scholars of race and racism have consolidated a dominant understanding of racism as an institutionalized set of practices and ideologies in which White privilege is jealously (if defensively) maintained. In such a system, racism is systemic and rational and is not simply located in an individual's prejudicial mindset and attitudes.[4] One of the most influential recent insights about contemporary racism is that it is "color blind" and thereby works to undermine legitimate claims of racism, which become difficult to pinpoint and prove.[5] One of the key characteristics of color-blind racism is the avoidance of explicitly racial language and conceptions, at the same time that racial practices remain subtly embedded in the normal operations of institutions.[6] Thus, racial inequalities continue to be reproduced, despite the many legal protections officially in force.

Rather than resorting to the now politically unacceptable language of innate racial differences, the (usually) less charged references to cultural and religious differences are often used as a coded means of racializing "others," and in particular Muslims, in Britain (as well as throughout many European countries), who are typically depicted as holding values that are inimical to the democratic and modern values of the West. Unfortunately, this study was unable to recruit more than a small number of South Asian/White participants (19), and most of these were professional middle-class individuals; thus narratives about anti-Muslim experiences are muted in this study. This is not to discount the extent to which anti-Black prejudice and discrimination continue to persist in Britain—as will be documented in the narratives of our multiracial participants below. However, among the younger generations of Britons (of all racial backgrounds), dating and partnerships with Black people generally no longer constitutes a major social transgression. This is borne out in the relatively high rates of especially younger male Black Britons who partner with White female Britons (and to a lesser extent, Black women partnered with White men).[7]

Despite the plethora of studies on racism and its many manifestations, most of this literature presumes that those who are negatively affected by racism(s) are monoracial minority people. Thus, we still know very little about the status and experiences of multiracial people within societies that are stratified along racial lines. Related bodies of literature, such as studies of "colorism" in the United States, have highlighted the variations in skin color and physical attributes even within so-called races, as well as the ways in which differences in skin color are associated with forms of disadvantage and inequality.[8]

In terms of how other people regard multiracial people, Mary Campbell and Melissa Herman found that about half of monoracial minority Americans and most White Americans believed that multiracial Americans should not be the beneficiaries of anti-discrimination policies—though the authors found that the multiracial people they surveyed reported similar levels of discrimination as monoracial minorities.[9] In fact, Herman found that Black/White adolescents in the United States perceived there to be just as much discrimination against them as their Black counterparts.[10] Likewise, Nikki Khanna found that many of the Black/White mixed people she interviewed believed that, in many contexts, they were seen just as negatively as other Black people.[11]

The few studies that have explored the negative racial experiences of multiracial people have focused primarily upon the experiences of Black/White multiracial people, though there is now some research in the United States that addresses the specific racialization of mixed people with various Asian ancestries.[12] In a recent Pew survey of the United States, a majority (55 percent) of multiracial respondents reported that they had been subjected to racial slurs or jokes. Significantly more Black/White people surveyed reported poor service in public places (like restaurants) and being stopped by the police, compared to Asian/White and Native American/White individuals.[13] As in the studies noted above, Black/White and Asian/White multiracial people reported levels of discrimination similar to those of Black and Asian people, respectively. In Britain, there has been no survey of the multiracial population comparable to the Pew survey in the United States.

There are a number of ways that multiracial people's experiences of racial prejudice and discrimination can be consequential. For instance, interactions in which an individual experiences a negative attitude or behavior toward his or her minority ancestry can reinforce identification with that ancestry; in such cases, race can be more salient to the individual than for those who do not feel racially stigmatized.[14] For Black/White and other types of multiracial individuals, racial rejection and racial hostility from co-ethnic minority people may also be an issue[15]—though such attitudes on the part of co-ethnics do not have the same dynamics as "racism."[16]

Do Multiracial Parents Feel Racially Stigmatized or "Othered"?

Before we explore whether multiracial parents were concerned about their children being subject to forms of racial prejudice, discrimination, or marginalization and how they tried to address such concerns, we turn to the question of whether our participants experienced forms of racial denigration themselves, either in the past or in the present. This question is important in itself, since we wondered how and to what degree parents' negative racial experiences could influence their thinking about their own children, as well as lead to a concern that they, too, could be racially denigrated or targeted.

In their reply to our question, only 10 (of 62) participants reported that they had *never* experienced forms of racial stigma or discrimination. Of these individuals, most (though not all) reported that they had always been seen as phenotypically White and had not been singled out as visibly different from their White peers. More commonly, 27 (of 62) parents reported that while many of them had encountered negative racial interactions growing up, especially at school (though the severity of this could differ considerably), they no longer felt that "it was an issue" in their day-to-day lives. Despite the fact that many of these participants were still aware of the possibility that they could be racialized in negative ways, they did not feel that this was an ongoing concern that required much thought or energy.

For instance, Joe (Black/White, 49), who grew up only with his White English mother in a semi-rural setting, reported that his gradual awareness of being seen as a Black boy in an almost exclusively White setting had been difficult during his childhood and teenage years. And although he still registered that he was seen as racially "different," he no longer experienced his awareness of his racial otherness in a way that was constant or oppressive, in part because he now felt very comfortable "in [his] own skin" as a mixed Black/White person—and one for whom race was not always salient. When asked if he felt subject to forms of racism, he replied:

> Hard question. . . . I would say that I feel racialized, even though I don't have a very strong racial identity. I'd say that I generally reject the idea of race, but I do feel as though I am seen as different and do feel different from other English people because of my physical appearance.

One relatively common theme among participants who reported that they no longer felt racially stigmatized was that they saw a lessening of distance and/or conflict between their various racial backgrounds, in comparison with the past. For many, any such schisms or conflicts were now resolved, usually through their identifying themselves as a multiracial person. Social psychologists studying the ways in which multiracial people manage their different racial backgrounds and identifications have found that the perception of a greater level of racial distance and conflict among a person's racial ancestries was associated with more racial stressors than for those who perceived little or no distance and conflict among their parental ancestries. So individuals with "high identity integration" tend to see their multiple racial backgrounds and identifications as largely compatible and complementary, while those with "low identity integration" see their ancestries as more oppositional and keep them more separate.[17]

While 27 (of 62) participants reported that racism was not a significant issue in their own lives, an almost equal number (25 of 62) reported
that they *still* felt somehow racially marked or stigmatized as adults—
though the degree to which they felt this way and the contexts in which
they experienced this, again, varied. Thus, some participants reported a
heightened awareness of being racially stigmatized through specific interactions with White people. For example, Serena (South Asian/White,
38), who lived in a predominantly White city in the South East, spoke of
how she has never felt accepted in Britain because of the presumption
on the part of others that she was foreign, or "Asian" (which in the British context, usually referred to people from the Indian subcontinent),
because she had black hair and fairly dark skin. Serena reported that her
colleagues in a former workplace always made "little snipey remarks":

And one of the girls [co-workers] said, "Oh he [referring to a young boy
in preschool] likes you because you look like a family member." I was like
right, okay. And then . . . and then we were all sitting there at . . . at . . .
at lunchtime, and she said, "Oh I bet Serena cooks a good chilli," and
like . . . and I was, "Oh why is that, because I'm brown?" Do you know
what I mean?'

Others frequently saw her as foreign in her day-to-day life:

Yeah. Well I just don't feel worthy of being British because I don't look it
and people don't treat me like I am. You know, like I think I might have
told you actually when it was . . . I think it was the World Cup or something . . . and some man said, "Ooh are you supporting our country?" and
I just thought oh! [Laughs]. You know, and I get that everywhere I go.

Of the 25 (16 women, 9 men) participants who reported feeling racially
stigmatized, 16 were of Black/White mixed ancestry—though of course
Black/White people also constituted the largest number of people (32) in
the sample. In other words, half of the Black/White respondents in this

sample reported that they still felt racially stigmatized as adults. And while some East Asian/White and South Asian/White participants continued to feel subject to forms of racial prejudice or discrimination from White people, East Asian/White participants in particular articulated anxieties about racial rejection and/or hostility from East Asian co-ethnics, who often did not regard part Asian people as "one of them."[18] Nor was it uncommon for our Black/White participants to report that they had encountered hostility from Black people because they were mixed and/or because they had partnered with a White person. For instance, Louise (Black/White, 44) described a harrowing incident with a Black neighbor:

> We did have an issue with a [Jamaican] neighbor who's now downstairs who we had one of those very public, council estate rows, and she ended up saying to me, "You're just a half-breed, you and your yellow bastard." So I don't know if she considers him [her son] a "yellow bastard," I know she certain considers me "just a half-breed."

Are the Children of Multiracial People Subject to Racism?

Did our multiracial parents think their children were (or will be) subject to racial stigma? One relevant observation is that while only 10 participants reported that they themselves had never experienced racism growing up (or ever), far more (38) participants reported that their children had never experienced it (or did not anticipate that they would, if they were very young). While 14 of 62 reported that they did not know if they had either because they had not spoken with their children about it or because their children were too young to be able to say that they had, 10 of 62 reported that some or all of their children had experienced racism. Although it is possible that some of the children (at least those who were old enough) may have disagreed with their parents' assessments, those were based, in part, upon discussions that they had had with their children, so that they had some sense of the ways in which other people saw and interacted with them at school, for example. In this regard, I relied upon parents' reports of their children's observed race—that is, how they were seen, racially, by others.

While participants who still felt racially targeted were more likely to express concern about their children being negatively racialized, that was not always the case. For instance, while Serena felt racially "othered" and was all too aware of how other people could see her as both "Muslim" and foreign on the basis of her appearance, she said that it never occurred to her that her children (whose father was White) would be vulnerable, because they looked entirely White to her and to others. Therefore, those parents who still felt subject to forms of racism appeared to be, on the whole, more attune to the possibility that their children, too, could be negatively perceived or treated—but only if they believed that their children looked non-White (which could include appearing racially ambiguous) to others.

On the whole, even among participants with White partners, first-generation Black/White participants were less likely to report that their children were seen as White by others, in comparison with South Asian/White and East Asian/White participants—a finding that meshes with those of most North American studies. While more than half the South Asian/White and East Asian/White parents reported that their children were seen as White, only a quarter of the Black/White parents did so—though this group included a small number of second-generation Black/White participants whose children reportedly appeared White. Not surprisingly, participants with non-White partners did not report that their children looked White.

Importantly, it was not uncommon for participants to report differences in how their *individual children* were seen by others, so that while some children looked White to others, others did not.[19] This issue of physical appearance, especially in relation to the variable phenotype of parents and children spoke to the extent to which racial uniformity and resemblance among family members can be taken for granted. Luke (Black/White, 48) spoke of the almost visceral alarm and disgust that some people could display when they saw him with his White mother:

Yeah, if I'm walking along with my mother with her shopping, people sort of . . . they . . . because she's this white haired white lady, you know, and she's walking along chatting to me and they see me give her a kiss and you know, "See you later," and I go, "Mum," they go [makes an expression of disgust] just like that.

Such discomfort (and even disgust) with the realization that parents and children did not resemble each other, racially, could register, both up and down the generations. Where Luke experienced other people's negative reactions to a visibly Black man calling an elderly White woman "mum," some parents were all too aware that their White-looking children could be stigmatized or bullied for having a parent who was visibly not White. For instance, Luke reported that his teenage daughter said, "Hi, Dad," very deliberately at school, so that people would know that he was her father (as she looked "Spanish" according to Luke, while he was seen as Black). He also spoke of how his son's peers' realization that his father was part Black had resulted in these boys harassing his son:

My son was in year seven [usually aged 11 or 12]. . . . His friends. Yeah. They was going, "Oh, your dad's a coon," and things like that and it was really making him uncomfortable but he'd sort of brush it off but at home he . . . his mum [Luke is remarried] phoned me, he was in floods of tears, he [was] really upset so . . . Where we used to drop the little one off at my wife's parents it's on his route and all the friends [were there] . . . and I got out the car . . . and I sort of said, "You all right Mark?" and I looked at his friends and smiled at them all and they . . . they was like [makes an uncomfortable and scared expression] because I'm not small. . . . Because I said, "Are these your friends?" and they was all like "mmmmmmmm."

Thus, when the children of our participants had parents or siblings who did not look White by prevailing social norms, parents worried that their children could be racially targeted. Gina (Black/White, 44), for one, felt this way about her children, despite their White appearance:

I suppose sometimes I worry that my kids would get picked on because of me, because I look different. Whereas they don't, they are very pale-skinned, they look White, to look at them they look White, but they are mixed race, I suppose, when I think about it. Like this has made me think about it, doing this, it's like, "Well they are [mixed race]," but they look White. So I worry that kids would get mean looking at me, like "Your mum's not White," but as far as I'm aware they've not had anyone say nothing to them, so I'm quite relieved.

Gina's experience notwithstanding, other White-looking children could be indirectly subject to racism when in the presence of a multiracial parent who did not look White. Brenda (Black/White, 44) described such an incident:

One situation was on a bus in [N] . . . I had [her son] in the pram, I had the girls with me, and as we'd got on we'd hit this old man's foot with the buggy, obviously by accident, and he was quite aggressive and said we should go back to where we came from. . . . I don't drive, the bus driver knew us. He stopped the bus and he demanded the bloke apologize, or get off the bus. And the man actually got banned from going on the buses because of that incident but the girls were with me and they experienced it. And we discussed it obviously and said sometimes that's how people are. . . . Not everybody is nice all the time. . . . People see a different color of skin. . . . They don't think it's very nice sometimes, but that's the minority and the majority of people especially in . . . most times now pretty much where ever you go is multicultural these days. . . . So . . . you just learn to live with it.

Rather than avoiding the topic, many of our participants tried to normalize discussion of skin color and other phenotypical differences and to acknowledge differences in physical appearance in the safe space of the home. In addition to reinforcing the idea that differences in physical appearance among family members were completely normal, such discussions could provide an opportunity for parents to create a positive self- image for their children, as Tanya (Black/White, 34), a mother of children aged 7, 4, and 1, observed:

> We talk about being brown. And we compare. . . . I talk about myself as being brown, and myself as being mixed race. . . . I suppose sometimes I talk about myself as being Black. . . . But generally we just keep it to trying to have an accurate self-image of what they actually are. And why that is—because some of our family comes from Jamaica, and some of our family come from Ireland and Scotland, that sort of thing. And I call it "mixed race."

Cases in which siblings were perceived as racially disparate, either in terms of skin color/gradations of lightness-darkness or in terms of particular "ethnic" features that were ascribed to the multiracial parent brought their own sets of concerns. For example, Evelyn (South Asian/ White, 43) had a son who appeared White and a daughter who was was much darker than her brother. When asked if her daughter had ever spoken to Evelyn about her appearance or looking different from her brother, Evelyn replied:

> Not really. . . . I point out that they're different in that, you know . . . I might say, "Steven, you've caught the sun," because he goes brown very, very quickly. And then . . . he'll go, "Let me see" (Evelyn mimes them comparing arms), and then Zoey will come along and I said, "Oh well, Zoey's darker like me isn't she?." So . . . I sort of say it in those terms so that it's there . . . in the conversation.

Participants such as Evelyn found it important to acknowledge physical differences between their children, even if indirectly, so that their children felt able to engage in a conversation about these differences if and when they wanted to.

Another parent, Cecilia (East Asian/White, 31), wondered about the possibility that her children will be perceived differently in racial terms, as they grew up:

> I was thinking maybe they might start asking why they have different color skin as well because it's so different. My son is very, very white, and my daughter's quite dark and in the sun she goes black, almost, so they might be perceived differently as they grow up.

Sometimes, differences in the racial appearance of individual members could engender questions about family relatedness and their belonging in the family, especially if one child was physically unlike her or his siblings. Elise's five children all looked slightly different from each other in terms of race, due to skin color and hair type. Elise (Black/White, 44) said that her youngest daughter, Emma, and her oldest, Jess, were both most commonly seen as White, while the other three children were more likely to be seen as Black, since they had darker skin like their mother. Here, Elise discusses how Emma perceived herself in relation to the rest of her family:

> ELISE: Emma's seven, her [White] father and I split up when she was three. . . . When she got to about five I don't know whether it was significant because she started school . . . but my [three middle children] live at home, [and] my other daughter Jess [who is seen as White] left home when she was about nineteen . . . I think [Emma] found it, the fact that she looked different to [sic] us, I think she sort of struggled with the fact that she didn't feel that she fitted in with the family.
>
> INT: So the only other one who looked mostly White, Jess . . .
>
> ELISE: Wasn't around . . . and obviously [her father] wasn't around.
>
> INT: When you say that you think she struggled with that a bit how did that manifest itself?

ELISE: Just by saying that she looked different, and it [was] obviously in her language. . . . And I obviously just reassured her that, you know, she's part of our family, and, I got some books actually about racial difference and that sort of helped her I think as well.

INT: So . . . because your daughter raised this issue with you quite explicitly even though she is very young, you responded to her by then addressing the issue explicitly as well. Did you find it difficult to talk to her about these issues, or not?

ELISE: No, I never. Because I've always been quite open with my children.

Here, the impact of changes in family and household composition is clear. Since Emma's White father was not present in their household, Emma did not have a parent whom she resembled, racially, and she did not see herself reflected in her family members, most of whom were much darker. Thus, Elise had to manage the issues that arose around race and family resemblance in a context in which the wider societal norm was that all members of a family looked alike. As illustrated here, an investigation into whether multiracial people are concerned about the ways in which their children may be racialized requires a disaggregation of the family unit, given the commonality of physical differences among siblings and between parents and children.

However, some participants' concerns about the possibility that their children could be racially targeted were allayed by several factors. These included class privilege, living in a middle-class neighborhood, and the sense of "changing times," which made them feel that they and their children were insulated from overt forms of racial prejudice or discrimination. Clare (Black/White, 43) had grown up in a working-class household with a Black Caribbean father and White British mother. She had some strong recollections about the racial abuse that she and both of her parents experienced when she was growing up, but as someone who now lived in an affluent part of London with a professional White British husband, Clare did not anticipate that her children would have such experiences:

> Yeah, well I think . . . I hope they feel positive and the reason I think they do is because, because so many of their friends are mixed and so they're amongst so many peers and they've got so many good experiences of that—their parents and these mixed-race kids are part of strong positive families. . . . When I was a kid . . . basically, the women were "White trash" if they went with Black men. . . . You know. Mixed-race kids were on par with gypsies. . . . But there is none of that association now, you know. Lauren's best friend is mixed race. Her dad is so rich he doesn't even have to work. The mum is an accountant, you know . . . and you know we're not part of "the scum of society" or any of that.

What is striking for participants who are now comfortably middle class and "respectable" are their scorching memories of feeling that mixed people had been regarded as "the scum of society." In Clare's case, as in those of many of the middle-class and educated participants in this study, wider normative changes (especially in middle-class neighborhoods and circles) regarding ethnic and racial diversity fundamentally affected how her children (and their many mixed peers) saw themselves as individuals who were not disadvantaged.

Generational Change and Greater Racial Awareness

The interviews with our participants revealed a strong theme regarding parents' need and obligation to demonstrate racial awareness for their children and to manage often subtle forms of racial denigration. While many of the parents in this study grew up during a time when overt forms of racial abuse and hostility became increasingly rare,[20] they were also aware of a "new racism"[21] and thus of the possibility that their children could be subject to instances of racial exclusion, marginalization, or denigration in specific settings or interactions, even with their friends and wider peer groups. As brilliantly discussed by Les Back in his study of South London youth clubs and racisms, young people appear to deconstruct and deny racial difference, at least temporarily, in multiethnic settings: "We are all the same around here" was a common mantra in that London youth club: "In a sense, the rejection of the significance of 'colour' constitutes an attempt to shrink the definition of inclusion and exclusion to a size that mirrors their immediate set of social relations. The nation is thus shrunk to the size of the neighbourhood, resulting in the emergence of a kind of 'neighbourhood nationalism.'"[22] Yet, as many parents came to realize, their children, especially those who did not look incontrovertibly White to others, could be vulnerable to situations in which they were perceived to be racially different, even in settings where they were usually deemed to belong.

A number of participants recalled how their own parents had adopted a philosophical attitude toward racist behavior or had to "turn the other cheek" in earlier decades. Luke (Black/White, 48) recalled conversations and interactions with his now-deceased father:

> My dad was brilliant at handling racism. Dad . . . We was walking down the street and I remember a guy called him a . . . like, "Nigger, get out of my way," and my dad . . . my dad just stepped to the side and gave him the biggest smile and said, "Certainly Sir." Luke recalled that his father then told him, "Don't give them people the time of day."

Luke was full of admiration for his father's forbearance and wit. But as someone who still felt subject to forms of racial prejudice, he knew that he himself could never respond in the way that his father had done. Rather, Luke reported that he would confront and challenge such behavior.

Victor's Black/White mixed father never talked about his experience of racist incidents, but his White Irish mother was overtly protective on her children's behalf.

I think at times my mum was very proud of who we were, and that we were mixed. My dad, he grew up in an era when you had to turn the other cheek to racism, that it was socially acceptable. While my mum would fight tooth and nail to defend us. . . . My dad . . . he went to work, he took your money. . . . I'm sure there are demons that he deals with but he would never talk to us. Very much just deal . . . , he would cope with it.

While some participants' minority parents had adopted a philosophical and resigned attitude toward others' prejudices (as in the cases above), others reported that when they told their parents about negative racial interactions, the responses had been almost unsympathetic. As Louise (Black/White, 44) recalled:

It would have been nice for me to have a mixed-race parent when I had odd issues arising. I remember as a child telling my [White Irish] mum that somebody next door had called me "blackie," [and] my mother's answer was "Well, they can't call you 'whitey,'" and I was sent back out again. And that was it, simple, in other words, "Go away, leave me alone, I'm busy. . . . Is that the worst your day can throw at you? Go back outside."

Other participants had similar experiences. For instance, Elaine (Black/White, 32) believed that the fact that her mother was White and of an older generation was significant in explaining how her mother had dealt with Elaine's difficulties around being a visibly Black woman:

Like I never really felt that my [White] mum, growing up, understood. She was just, "Oh, you are who you are," you know, "It doesn't . . . doesn't matter. Sticks and stones will . . ." you know, all of that sort of thing, you know, to cover over everything but didn't really understand that because like my . . . my identity was quite visible, that actually I needed to understand that part of my identity and my mum didn't understand it and she didn't go out and learn anything about it to teach me. . . . And therefore I didn't have any kind of ammunition . . . or anything to be proud of or anything to understand and so yeah, I think . . . I thought that was quite . . . quite hard.

Likewise, Rachel (South Asian/White, 51) felt aggrieved about the fact that her parents had failed not only to prepare her for the harsh racial realities she encountered while growing up, but also to expose her to her mother's Asian ancestry and background:

> I feel very strongly about my mother—that she always had a duty to take us back to Malaysia while me and my sister were little but . . . I might sound very critical now but I think because . . . we had no sense of identity of being Malaysian, and because . . . we experienced a lot of racism, I think . . . there was a moral obligation almost on my mother to take us to Malaysia to show us what it was all about, and show us our heritage, and help us really to cope with living somewhere where we were so unusual. But she never took us.

Not wanting her daughters to experience the alienation, marginalization, and racism that she had, Rachel felt very strongly that her daughters should know about their Indian Malaysian heritage and that it was her responsibility to impart it.

While many of our participants, especially those who were Black/White, had reflected upon the possibility that their own children could be subjected to forms of racial prejudice, stereotyping, and discrimination, they were prepared to be much more willing than their own parents to discuss negative racial experiences with their children, as well as to address these issues preemptively. In fact, some of the participants were extremely proud that their children displayed confidence when talking about or confronting racism, especially in comparison to how they themselves might have coped with such issues when they were growing up. As Elise (Black/White, 44) put it:

> I think they're so aware. . . . They're more aware than we were, . . . My generation when we were younger, growing up, about racism . . . covert rac-

ism and stuff like that, and they are really switched on with stuff. So, they won't have any of it, they just address it, whereas I probably . . . at their age . . . I probably wouldn't have had the confidence to maybe have addressed it. . . . I think you have to address it, you know, people's attitudes.

Elaine (Black/White, 32), too, spoke proudly of her son's willingness to confront racism when he was with his White grandmother and his grandmother's brother's family:

Like he was at my uncle's house last year and noticed the Golliwog [a Black rag doll popular in the past] on the top of a shelf. I wasn't there and my mum . . . he was with my mum, and he's just very vocal with all of our family in the room and was saying, "Whose Golliwog is that up there? Do they know that that is racist?" . . . and made this really big thing about it and my mum was trying to get him to be quiet.

Later in the interview, she reflected some more on this incident:

But it was just interesting that he, for the first time, spotted it and outed it and my mum was trying to get him to be quiet so as not to start a family argument.

While many parents realized that they were raising their children at a time and in a place where overt manifestations of racism were socially taboo, they were aware of "low level" potentially racist scenarios that did not usually involve an easily identifiable racist moment or act.[23] Some parents pointed to rising anti-immigration discourses and how young people (especially those who did not appear White) could be caught in the midst of xenophobic sentiments and interactions. Even if they (or their children) were not the intended targets of racial or ethnic prejudice/hostility, they were at times offended and uneasy when people made racist or xenophobic comments about others.

Fostering Racial Awareness and Inclusivity

For many of the parents who took part in our study, fostering racial awareness was an important part of how they socialized their children (see Chapter 3). The motivations for doing so were varied and did not have solely to do with concerns about protecting their children from negative racial encounters. That is, even parents (especially those who adopted a cosmopolitan ethos of parenting) who did not think their children were vulnerable to negative forms of racialization could make efforts to foster an awareness and appreciation of ethnic diversity, as part of an attempt to instill a broad-minded sense of racial inclusion and acceptance of others.

Fostering racial awareness involves a recognition that the perception of ethnic and racial difference has real and material effects in our interactions and daily lives and is at odds with a "color-blind" perspective, in which people may deny the continuing consequences of race and racialized systems/structures.[24] According to Kerry Anne Rockquemore and Tracey Laszloffy, "Traditionally, racial socialization refers to the ways in which black parents teach their children about the realities of race. Racial socialization includes preparing them to manage situations where racial discrimination occurs, and fostering positive beliefs about their racial identity to counter societal devaluation."[25] While this conceptualization was formulated in relation to African Americans in the United States, it also resonates with what our British Black/White participants said about the socialization of their children.

Many parents found themselves caught between feeling that they were responsible for preparing their children (especially those who did not look White) for the possibility of negative racial interactions and at the same time, feeling that they did not want to impose their concerns about racism onto their children. As Clare (Black/White, 43) explained,

> The fact is I'm aware that even though sometimes I seem to make a big deal of race, in fact there is no . . . the fact is when you're talking to kids

of this age [seven and eleven] they're almost like, "Race, what race?" It's almost like you're trying to impose something [on them] that's unimportant, yeah, bring something up that they haven't even thought about.

The parents in this study engaged with their children about racial awareness either by discussing specific moments or experiences of racial abuse, discrimination, or "gate-keeping" /exclusion, or by emphasizing inclusivity and respect for diversity, or both. However, some parents were more proactive than others in doing so. Typically, many parents engaged in strategic discussions about race and difference when the opportunities arose—for example, when watching television together, or hearing a news report about an incident, or any other interaction that occurred in their daily lives. Some parents sought to preempt issues or problems related to physical appearance by explicitly talking about appearance, while others waited until children raised it as an issue themselves. Comments about a child's appearance or the child's own observations about his or her appearance, in relation to others, often acted as a trigger for discussions of racial identity and heritage.

Responding to Specific Racial Incidents

Specific moments of racial abuse or discrimination (or ones that felt racial, albeit somewhat ambiguously) either toward the child or the parent (in the company of the child) could often act as an impetus for explicit discussions within the family about racial awareness and assessing the nature of racial interactions. Various parents spoke about *that* moment of self-realization, when children who were previously unaware of any concept of racial difference or what "color," "Black," or "White" meant suddenly became aware that they were somehow "different."

For instance, Tanya (Black/White, 34) was very upset when her 4-year-old son came home from nursery school saying that a White child, Henry, had said he didn't want to play with him because his "face was strange" and that "he didn't like [him] because [he] was orange."

Here Tanya talks about how she spoke to her son about other people's views and impressed upon him the subjectivity (and incorrectness) of other people's projections and pronouncements about his racialized body:

> Once I'd calmed down [after the incident] . . . we talked about it straight away, a couple of times, about how "poor Henry, he doesn't really understand that God made us all differently, and that how I am is exactly how God meant me to be" and that "this is our color, look, aren't we beautiful?" and "My skin's beautiful, is your skin beautiful?" "Yes, it is." "Are we beautiful?" "Yes, we are." And . . . "Poor Henry, he can't quite see how beautiful we are, we're sorry for Henry," and all this sort of thing. . . . I suppose I try to equip them with the sense that "who is Henry anyway?," do you know what I mean? I try and help them to see that if someone calls you a chair, does it make you a chair? I don't know, but I try to instill in them not to take other people's shit on, is what I'm trying to say. But it was really difficult, I did feel quite stumped. Because you just think, "Oh my god, this is one of those key moments, am I going to fuck it up, or am I going to say the right thing?" And it's really hard, it's really hard.

It is clear that the decision to tackle this issue with her son in such a way was not an easy one—that instead it was fraught with questions of how and when to deal with it, and what the lasting effects might be on his self-esteem, his racial identity, and sense of self. As Tanya points out, there is no "how to" manual for handling such scenarios with young children. Here, Tanya adopts a creative and empowering approach of feeling sorry for the other child, suggesting that he behaved the way he did because of ignorance and a lack of understanding—and indirectly that the fault was not his, but rather that of the family and the society in which he was growing up.

Diane (East Asian/White, 54) talked of how her daughter Rita had confided in her about getting "racist insults" as a teaching assistant from some secondary school pupils—which is to say that multiracial parents' interactions with their children around issues of race can continue into their adulthood. Her daughter looked rather "Chinese" even though she was second-generation mixed, with a White father.

> But she [daughter] did report it and I advised her to report it as well because, you know, it's not . . . obviously it's wrong, it's not acceptable. . . . So I mean yeah, we have talked a bit about how it feels and what . . . what you can say and, you know, how you . . . how you need to say it's not acceptable, you know, not just accept it.

Parental support with racial awareness can continue through the life course and include situations relating to partners and interactions with a partner's family members. Joanna (Black/White, 57) spoke of an incident that had been very upsetting for her son:

> My son who does look mixed race, he had no problems . . . because he had lots of mixed-race friends and he has Black friends and White friends until he got a girlfriend when he was, I think, about twenty . . . interestingly enough whose father was from Corsica and had come here as an immigrant in the fifties and must have experienced a lot of racism. The mother is White and they said they weren't . . . they wouldn't have my son in the house because he was mixed race. Can you believe this? . . . And they didn't believe that he was [mixed race] . . . that his father was White. . . . I mean it was just like totally mind-blowing to me and he was really upset by it of course. Anyway, we talked about that. We discussed that and what the motivation might be for that from their parents.

A number of parents also spoke of incidents that arose in their children's schools and peer groups—when their children's peers realized that they had non-White parents. Joanna (Black/White, 57) reported:

> My daughter was told by a group of Black girls in her secondary school, they didn't know she was mixed race until I went to pick her up—it's not

clear when you see my daughter that she is mixed race—and they saw me and realized that she was and this group of Black girls said to my daughter [that] she was to choose—was she going to be friends with the White girls or the Black girls? That really made me furious and we had a discussion about it at that point and I said, "No, you're not going to choose. You know, why should you choose? You choose your friends by the people that they are, not by the color of their skins."

In other cases, some children could be subject to forms of racial gatekeeping by monoracial minority peers who let them know that they were not seen as "one of them." For instance, Sophie (Black/White, 31) reported an incident with her son:

The other day somebody said to him, "You're not Jamaican," and he said, "Yeah, my dad is," and they said "No, you're not, you're White," and he said, "No I'm not actually, I'm mixed," and he [the other boy] said, "Well, mixed isn't a color." So he said to me, "Mum . . ." and I said to him, "Oh, stupid people, they don't know what they're talking about, it's your identity, and that's that." . . . But I do worry, because I think they might not know what he is, or he might not know, and he might feel like he has to choose.

Thus, the policing of group boundaries and membership, and who can or cannot claim a particular identity, was played out in discourses about racial authenticity (both on the basis of physical appearance or the demonstration of specific cultural attributes), notions of blood quantum and racial fractions, and racialized scripts of behavior to which children were expected to adhere.[26]

Black/White Participants and Everyday Education

As these excerpts illustrate, some parents encouraged their children to stand up against racism by calling people out on racist sentiments, language and acts and by rebuking and educating them, even in settings where their children were not the intended targets of racial prejudice or hostility. The Black/White participants, in particular, reported various ways in which they fostered racial awareness.[27] Many parents wanted their children to feel confident enough to be able to identify and contest forms of racism leveled against them or other "others," and they tried to instill such confidence and awareness through everyday discussions, as the opportunity arose.

Some participants also spoke of the importance of being assertive in interactions with others. For example, while Clare (Black/White, 43) let her children know that she was there to back them up in the face of any explicit racism, she also made a point of showing them how to carry themselves in interactions with other people or in encounters that were traditionally laden with power inequities:

> Lauren and Marcus would know that I would be there to fight their corner but more than that they've seen me talk to teachers on a level [where] I wouldn't be in a master-servant sort of "yes . . . whatever you say." And it's all this sort of thing . . . learning that they can just see, that I think is worth a lot. . . . What I am trying to do with the kids is just arm them so that they have a good sense of self and so that they have a good understanding of the issues so that they know that if they do come across, come up against this sort of bias which is really insidious, really difficult to sort of . . . sort of pinpoint as racist or whatever . . . they've got the wherewithal to overcome these sort of difficulties.

In comparison with the other participants in this study, Black/White parents (who comprised about half the number of respondents) exhibited a prominent consciousness about the legacy of racial histories and tended to speak of concerted efforts to address the history of Black enslavement and/or Black civil rights. While many of the East Asian/White and South Asian/White participants reflected upon the dynamics of cultural "dilution" and disconnection from their Asian ancestors, they did not articulate a strong racial consciousness in the ways that many Black/

White participants did. Given that the threat of social injustice and racial strife has historically been a prominent part of many Black people's experiences and consciousness (certainly in North America, but also in countries such as Britain), confronting racism may in itself be an important part of Black cultural heritage and socialization.[28]

Parents—and in particular Black/White parents—educated their children about historical institutions and periods of discrimination and racism, including slavery and the Holocaust. Many of these parents used films, books, and television programs to tie in their lessons with what the children were studying at school. According to Anna (second-generation Black/White, 44),

> It's not like we talk about it all the time, because we don't, but if we are reflecting . . . or it comes up in conversation I will make a link. . . . I will say, "Just imagine how that might have felt for . . . great-granddad when he came here." . . . In the summer we went to the . . . Municipal Museum in Bordeaux and there's a huge exhibition there about slavery, and we did explicitly talk about the fact [that] somewhere . . . there will probably be somebody that we're related to who had this experience in some way, shape or form. . . . Certainly for [her son] that was pretty challenging. . . . He found that really quite shocking and quite stark and he was quite troubled by it. . . . I'm not . . . quite sure why I do it apart from I think they should know and they should understand it's not that many steps away from their life and it could have been very, very different.

This discussion was especially meaningful for Anna because both of her children looked White, and their Black ancestry, in terms of generational lineage, was quite removed. So while Anna was not systematic in discussing these issues, it was important for her that she reminded her children of her maternal Black Caribbean heritage. Many of these Black/White parents also drew on examples of famous mixed-race people such as Barack Obama or the British race-car driver Lewis Hamilton as role models to show their children that mixed-race people can occupy influential and powerful positions in society and that a mixed heritage was something to be proud of. In this regard, it was notable that South Asian/White and East Asian/White participants had virtually no public figures or roles models who were known to be "mixed" with their heritages.

Conclusion

Although a little less than half the participants no longer felt that they were subject to negative racial interactions (though they had been while growing up), the other half still felt racially marked in a variety of negative ways, though to different degrees—especially in the case of Black/White participants and a small number of South Asian/White and East Asian/White participants. Nevertheless, over half the participants in our study said they believed that their children were not or would not be subject to forms of racial prejudice or discrimination, and the primary reason underlying this belief was their children's White appearance. Because 46 (of 62) participants had White partners with whom they had had children, a significant number of the South Asian/White and East Asian/White participants had children who appeared White (as did a smaller number of Black/White participants, especially second-generation Black/White participants). So despite the growing appreciation for ethnic and racial diversification and its increasing commonality, our participants understood that the appearance of Whiteness afforded both status and protection for their children.

In comparison with their own upbringings, in which open discussion of negative racial experiences with their parents had been rare and in some cases, even discouraged, the participants in this study understood that in the current climate overt forms of racisms were relatively uncommon. Nevertheless, many parents remained alert to the very real possibility that their children could be subtly marginalized or stigmatized by their very relatedness to their parents, for instance, when their children were seen with them in public places such as schools.

While some parents were uncertain about how to socialize their children or bring in lessons about racial awareness or history, others had a very clear idea for how to do so. In addition to their broader racial histories, various cultural norms associated with specific groups could influence how these parents responded to and coped with instances of racial prejudice or discrimination.[29] Parents chose to teach their children on their own terms or in conjunction with what was being taught in schools. In their efforts to open up a safe space at home for children to ask questions, they also considered how age and developmental stage were important factors in their decisions about *when* and *how* to broach these subjects with their children. It is interesting that many—though not all—second-generation Black/White participants reported concerted efforts to create awareness of Black history for their children and to foster a sense of connectedness to it. It may be that the greater genealogical distance from their Black ancestry actually galvanized these participants to work at retaining and enlivening that link.

The finding that Black/White parents seemed to foster racial awareness more proactively than other mixed parents resonates with findings about the specificity of the Black or part-Black experience in the United States. It further suggests that, as various US analysts have argued,[30] some non-Black multiracial people who are sometimes seen as White and can enjoy forms of White privilege need not consciously address the role that race and the perception of racial difference can play in their lives. Nevertheless, some East Asian/White and South Asian/White participants who had been negatively racialized also expressed concerns about their children.[31] In comparison with our Black/White participants, some South Asian/White participants were primarily concerned about Islamophobic sentiments, which could be directed against them or their children, while the East Asian/White participants were more attune to forms of racial ridicule and racial stereotyping such as being taunted with "ching chong" or treated as "fresh off the boat migrants" who cannot speak English, which they believed were often not recognized as "real" racism.[32] Claire Jean Kim's theory of "racial triangulation," which posits that African Americans are often subject to attributions of racial inferiority, while Asian Americans are socially excluded as foreigners (and not seen as bona fide Americans), appears to apply to some extent in Britain, in relation to Black and Asian groups.[33]

Thus, much of what the parents in this British study reported supports findings in the United States concerning "color blind" racism and a growing awareness of White denial and pushback in the wider society. Nevertheless, the British case provides an interesting counterpoint to that of the United States, especially in terms of Black/White relations. In a timely article, Nancy Foner poses the question of whether Islam in Western Europe is like race in the United States, recognizing the predominantly negative portrayals of Muslims in Europe and the crystallization of societal discourses in which Muslims (usually South Asian in the case of Britain) constitute the truly problematic "other" in British society.[34] She concludes that the racial Black/White divide in the United States is less "permeable" than that of the religious divide concerning Muslims in Europe.

However, contemporary British discourses about problematic forms of "difference" are now heavily centered on the specter of (usually South Asian) Muslim extremism, given Britain's colonial past and the large numbers of Britons of Pakistani and Bangladeshi Muslim backgrounds.[35] Because only a small number of participants (19 of 62) in this study were South Asian/White and because many of them were non-Muslim, middle-class professionals, this study has not been able to gauge how the extent to which anti-Muslim sentiments may have impinged upon their lives. And while moral panics can be generated in relation to both Black and South Asian Muslim people, Black people in Britain are no longer regarded, on the whole, as *fundamentally* threatening to the civil and social order (though discourses about Black male criminality are still widespread).

Only time will tell whether non-White Muslims will be regarded as truly belonging in Britain. For now, various studies point to the social and economic disadvantages experienced by working-class Muslims.[36]

In comparison with many working-class Black Britons, a significant number of whom partner with White Britons, South Asian Muslims in Britain do not generally intermarry across racial and religious lines.[37] Black/White partnering and, more generally, "mixing" in friendship groups and local youth cultures, especially in urban areas throughout Britain, point to the increasingly normalized and unremarkable fact of Black/White interactions and unions and their widespread social acceptance.[38] Thus, while there are some aspects of the "black exceptionalism" thesis that apply to Britain—that is, while the wider public tends to see Black/White people as Black with more regularity than they see South Asian/White and East Asian/White people as monoracially South Asian and East Asian, respectively—there is also growing evidence that, in Britain, the racial divide between Black and White is gradually fading.

The parents in our study were highly alert to the fact that they lived at a time when overt forms of racial prejudice or discrimination were not socially acceptable and thus relatively rare, in comparison with more subtle forms of negative racial interactions and discourses. At the same time, as we will see in the next chapter, many of the multiracial parents in this study understood all too well that emergent incarnations and discourses of racial othering and prejudice could accompany a new era of "race relations" in increasingly diverse towns and cities throughout Britain.

5

The Future

"Dilution" and Social Change

In addition to the increasing numbers of interracial partnerships and mixed children, discourses about "mixing" can be a good barometer of how people conceive of increasing diversity and its implications for integration and the blurring of ethnic and racial boundaries. I wanted to see what parents thought about ethnic and racial difference in the future, and whether they thought that race and racial difference would continue to matter. First, many parents spoke about the future in terms of what would be in store for their children and their own family's role in the evolving make-up of British society, where they saw themselves and their children at the forefront of breaking down racial barriers. The mere fact that they and their children were mixed meant that they were part of a societal shift towards greater racial diversity. In this vein, parents often spoke about their children's possible future partners, the kinds of families they might create for themselves, and what the resulting reinforcement or "dilution" of mixture in their future families might bode for the demographics and societal norms in Britain more generally.

The second area of discussion concerned racial and ethnic difference, and whether, with the growth of the mixed population in Britain, conceptions of difference and race would continue to divide the wider society. Here, parents often drew upon their own experiences of being mixed race in Britain to ascertain whether or not things had changed for their children's generation, and if so, whether change was for the better, or worse. In general, parents felt that Britain today was a better place to grow up mixed, and many parents spoke of their pleasure at seeing their children live in a society that was much more accepting and diverse than they had experienced growing up. While there were certainly some concerns about specific experiences of racism (especially among parents with Black ancestry), or what they perceived to be a growing anti-immigration rhetoric from the Right, parents (especially those in diverse urban areas such as London) spoke about the ease with which their children lived alongside those from other backgrounds and about how rarely their children actually "saw" or thought about race when it came to their peers and their daily lives. That is, while awareness of race and ethnic diversity was still undeniably present, such diversity appeared to be a taken-for-granted feature of everyday life and interactions for many of our participants and their children.

Parents' Thoughts about Their Children's Future Partners

In exploring participants' thoughts about the future, we asked them if they had any ideas about, or preference for, their children's future partners, especially in terms of their ethnic and racial backgrounds. We anticipated that questions related to the race, ethnicity, and culture of their children's future partners might be on the minds of those who were mixed themselves. The majority of participants in this study had children who were not yet old enough to be in stable partnerships (though some were dating or in more long-term relationships). We encouraged parents to be as honest as possible, given the likelihood that many parents could feel uncomfortable about stating their true feelings on the subject, and indeed, all our participants seemed to be highly aware of the taboos around stating an ethnic or racial preference in terms of their children's partners. For some parents, views about their children's current or future relationships tended to be concerned with possible forms of racial abuse (especially if their children were to have White partners), or more commonly, thoughts about lineage and their feelings about continuity or loss of heritage and bloodlines.

Our parents realized that their own preferences were likely to play only a small part in their children's decisions about their choice of partner. Some parents also spoke about partnering as a natural evolution within their children's social network. For example, if they tended to socialize and identify with a mostly Black peer group, they were also likely to date within this group. A number of parents of older children saw their children as quite open-minded and internationally inclined, as they wanted to go to university and travel, and they anticipated that their children would enter into quite cosmopolitan partnerships and/or be with people who shared a similar mindset.

While the majority of participants (46 of 62) said that they had no preference whatsoever regarding their children's future partners, some parents indicated that they would be happy if their children partnered with someone who was not White or who shared some aspect of their minority ethnic heritage. Only a small number of parents spoke openly of a strong preference for their children to have either a White or non-White partner, though it is possible that others were not forthcoming on this issue. Parents offered a range of justifications for their preferences, which revealed their thinking about their children's ethnic and racial identifications, their own feelings about their minority heritage, their aspirations for their children, and the kinds of family lives they wanted for them. Parents' views about their children's partners also illuminated their feelings about the possibility of ethnic and racial "dilution," down the generations.

Parents Who Expressed No Preference at All

Perhaps not surprisingly, the majority of parents immediately stated that they had no preference at all regarding their children's partners. Josh (South Asian/White, 32) and his Black British partner, Alicia, were quite clear that "color" did not matter (theirs was the only joint interview in the study[1]):

JOSH: Doesn't matter.
ALICIA: They can be any colour, they can be gay, straight, don't care. As
    long as they're happy.

JOSH: I remember when I was growing up, my mum and dad said, "It doesn't matter who you marry, just as long as you're happy." Because I think they probably must have experienced it [hostility around their interracial partnership], not that they really talked about it that much, apart from obviously what I'd notice from other people, but yeah, they said to me and my sister as a child, "It doesn't matter, anybody, any race, it's just not important."

ALICIA: We're not fussed. As long as they're happy.

JOSH: No preference at all, any human is fine.

In this excerpt, both parents were quite adamant about not having a preference. At the end, Josh's statement that "any human is fine" suggests a racially transcendent, post-race discourse among these parents. The fact that Josh is South Asian/White and his wife is Black British (thus making them a minority mixed couple) may have reinforced their view that race and racial difference simply did not matter to them. Either way, their disavowal of the importance of race was central to how they saw themselves and themselves to others, since they were often the objects of curiosity in public settings. Interestingly, Josh refers to his parents' encouraging advice toward him, and in this way, he replicates the same stance that they had adopted.

Jonathon (East Asian/White, 42) was also very clear about not having any preference about his children's future partners:

I couldn't give a monkey's who they partner with, as long as they're happy and stable, that's the most important thing, so it wouldn't matter.

Garret (Black/White, 50) was also emphatic when asked if he had any preferences about his children's partners. "None whatsoever," he replied.

There are far more important things to be considered when entering into a relationship. I'd also like to say that beyond trying to counsel them if it was seen that they were walking into a "mistake," it's not really any of my business, though I would find it very hard to deal with someone who had immoral or oppressive political or religious beliefs.

Likewise, Joe (Black/White, 49) had no preference for his children's choice of partner, but acknowledged that his children (like most people) were likely to want to partner with people whose interests mirrored their own:

> I do think that identity is wrapped up in choice of partner and in quite complex ways. . . . You know . . . questions about the "exotic" and similarity and . . . particularly for people who are outward looking. . . . I mean, I always wanted to travel and [his wife] always wanted to travel so . . . I'm sure there's something about our choice of partner which is to do with . . . looking for something which is sort of similar and yet different. . . . And that's probably true for [his son] Stephen too, and his girlfriend's a Chinese specialist so she's just spent a year in . . . she's spent a year in Beijing . . . But in terms of wishing he was a bit more of one thing or another . . . I am definitely a kind of live and let live sort of person. He's twenty-two now so it feels kind of balanced and in terms of his identity, I don't know . . . I feel that they [sic] had space to be mixed in a way that I didn't.

Joe's thoughts on his children's partners touch on the fact that the contemporary recognition of being "mixed" in Britain has also engendered a more tolerant attitude toward a whole range of possible partnerships.

Rebecca (Black/White, 51) did not have any preference regarding her daughter's future partner, but she, like Josh, wanted someone who would be kind and good for her daughter:

> I don't have any problems with, if she married a lady, whatever, as long as she's happy, as long as she's not being disruptive or damaging herself in any way or they're damaging her in any way. These are the more important things for me, as long as she's successful and growing and living life

to the full, that's the most important thing. And I think she will choose whoever she wants to be with in that same respect.

Interestingly, many of the people who stated their complete lack of preference, such as Rebecca, above, often coupled this with saying that they wouldn't care if their child partnered with someone of the same sex—quite a big marker of cosmopolitanism and support for broader societal discourses of acceptance, diversity and equality.

In contrast to these parents, others drew upon their own (often negative) experiences to justify why they would prefer their children to partner with either "someone like them" or someone from the White "mainstream" in order to avoid cultural conflict, stigma, or racial discrimination.

Parents' Preference for Partners with a Specific Ethnic or Racial Heritage

Only a few parents expressed a clear preference about their children's partners, though their justifications for doing so varied. Alberto (South Asian/White, 39) was unique in explicitly stating that he wanted his daughter to partner with a White European person.

INT: Do you have any particular preference for the kind of person that [your daughter] would partner with?

ALBERTO: Yeah . . . I think she should try and marry someone European so that the children will be similar to her. They'll [their children] be similar, and to him. So someone European, even American's all right.

INT: So do you think that if you're not European in that situation that you're much more vulnerable to being stigmatized?

ALBERTO: No, it's not that. That's not the reason. It's just a lot easier if you have somebody that's like you. . . . If you marry someone that's from a completely different sort of background or different DNA, you're going to have somebody that looks nothing like you, might still look beautiful but look totally different.

Indicating that his daughter is seen as a White European and that he would like his daughter to partner with a White European man, Albert considers it to be a given that people want their children to look like them. As discussed in the chapter on racism, a lack of racial resemblance among parents and children (or between siblings) can lead to situations in which other people could make upsetting remarks, or even question their relatedness. When Alberto says that "it's just a lot easier if you have somebody that's like you," he also denies any suggestion that a White European status would be more advantageous to his daughter. This denial is interesting, because earlier in the interview, he spoke of how he had changed his South Asian surname to his mother's Spanish surname because he had felt disadvantaged when applying for jobs.

Pauline (East Asian/White, 55) also stated a preference for her daughters to partner with European individuals, though her emphasis fell more on her preference that they not partner with East Asians:

It will be European, I think European. I wouldn't want them to marry Chinese. I wouldn't want them to. . . . Because [of] the things that my mother has said, I don't think that Chinese men are particularly sensitive. I think my mother is pleased that she hasn't married a Chinese or Oriental person [and] from the talks that she's had with Japanese women as well, they're quite domineering. . . . They expect women to play their sort of stereotypical role, maybe the younger ones are slightly different but I think they're still expected to follow these sort of rituals . . . especially if they are from the mainland, if they are very traditional Chinese. They expect the traditions to keep going, you know.

Although she believed Chinese men to be overly traditional and patriarchal, and thus not suitable for her daughters, Pauline also expressed some ambivalence about her daughters partnering with European men, especially in terms of a loss of Chinese heritage and lineage.

In contrast to Pauline, Brian (South Asian/White, 33), who reported that he and his Japanese wife would prefer their son to partner with a Japanese or East Asian woman, emphasized that they would not want their son to marry a White Briton.

> I think it would probably be if it was anything I think me and [his Japanese wife] maybe would be more worried about [their son] being with a traditional White English girl because, not all, but you know many of the girls I don't know how to put this. Many of the girls I was with when I was younger were very selfish. And obviously for your kids it's not to do with skin color but it's about attitude really and I think we're becoming . . . a lot of people are becoming more individualistic, more materialistic.

Both of these participants articulated quite essentialist and negative views of "Chinese" men and "English" women, respectively, in explaining their preferences.

While the parents above stated clear preferences around future partners on the grounds of cultural pros and cons (and the "fit" between their children and a potential partner), other parents had strong views and feelings about retaining a consciousness of their minority heritage. For instance, Tara (Black/White, 50) stated that she hoped her daughters would partner with Black or part-Black men:

> Part of me thinks if they both have White partners then the color can be lost, like you know it can just disappear . . . as, as, as happened many times in the past in this country. . . . The reason it bothers me, I think no, I think what really bothers me is I don't want them to forget that race matters. That race affects people's life chances, that there is this hierarchy of shadeism—the lighter you are the better your life chances.

Later in the interview, Tara spoke of her discomfort with her daughter's choice of White partners:

> Like I feel uncomfortable that Lianne only goes out with White men. . . . I know it's to do with me and how she feels I've stuffed race down her throat . . . that there's a little bit of me that thinks [she] rejects her Blackness. I know deep down she doesn't. But, it's more a rejection of me, do you know what I mean?

Tara's strong wish that her daughters would partner with either mixed Black/White or Black partners was also influenced by the fact that her relationships with both of the White fathers of her daughters had ended badly—in large part, according to Tara, because of these White partners' latent racism toward her.

In her research on Black/White interracial unions in the United States, Erica Chito Childs found evidence that the family members of *both* Black and White individuals in interracial relationships could disapprove of their interracial unions, even though they denied that racial difference was, in fact, the basis for their opposition or "concern." According to her, family members (and the wider society) often employ a discursive strategy—"the problem of the children"—to rationalize their concern or discomfort. However, unlike White family members, who were mostly concerned to maintain White privilege by keeping their families entirely White, Black familial opposition was most often due to concerns about lingering (often hidden) forms of racism and a distrust of White people more generally.[2]

A few parents, like Victor (second-generation Black/White, 39), opposed the idea of a White partner for their child due to the possibility that a White partner's wider family could reject that child. Speaking of his son, Victor said,

> It's gonna be strange because once my son becomes that age, there are going to be so many origins in this country. I suppose in my mind I

wouldn't want him to be exposed to the pain of my, like, older brother. He dated a White girl and he wasn't allowed into the house.

Victor's protective stance toward his infant son, his desire to shield him from racial rejection and hostility, was combined with a strong sense of preserving and cultivating his father's Black Caribbean ancestry (his own father had little connection with it, having been raised without his Caribbean father), as well as his wife's Black African ancestry and culture.

Parents' Subtle Preferences

Wishes as explicit as Alberto's and Tara's were exceptional among participants, but many parents did, in other more subtle ways, express a preference regarding children's choice of partner in an ideal or imagined world (if it was up to them). Although most parents did not state a *strong* or overt preference, it did become evident that, when nudged, they would also be happy, or happier, if their children partnered with a person of a particular ethnic or racial background.

A number of parents expressed the wish that their children partner with someone who would revitalize their ethnic minority heritage. For example, Abike (Black/White, 58) initially reported that she had no preference, but then admitted that she would find it "odd" or "weird" and perhaps a bit sad to think that if her children, who had a White father, partnered with White people, *their* children would be "completely white":

It is interesting because Myles [her son] has lived for seven years or so with his partner Karen, who's Irish, and in some ways I often think she and I have got quite a bit in common because she feels a bit like an exile even though Ireland's not that far away. But I'm aware in the awful sort of way, almost like some horrible eugenicist, their children will be just, kind of, completely White. Which is kind of odd, I sort of think . . . and I don't know if he ever thinks about that. And Yeni [her daughter] will probably adopt and I think she'd adopt a mixed-race child, you know, she'd be in a good position to, one would hope. So . . . it will be kind of weird.

Responding in a different vein, several Black/White participants who reported that they did not mind who their children's partners were, later noted that they did not want their own children to partner with individuals who simply had a "thing" for Black people. Dennis (Black/White, 45) recalled his own experiences of dating White women:

> I suppose . . . one thing that I did miss out which I wouldn't want to happen to my sons as well, when I used to date White women when I was younger, the only White women I could date were the ones who'd just go out with black people. The stereotypical side. . . . If I could have got one that was with me for me then it would have been different, so I would say whoever they are with as long as they're with them for the right reasons and not for the color or stereotypical thing . . . I don't mind.

As Dennis discusses here, very poignantly, he would not want his sons to be racially objectified in the way he felt he had been, when he dated certain White women. He wanted his sons to have partners who appreciated them for who they were as individuals, not as Black men per se.

Some participants were reluctant to admit that they actually had a preference. These parents appeared embarrassed, or even guilty, about divulging a preference, especially if they had previously spoken about promoting acceptance and cosmopolitanism in their own family lives. They may have felt that by admitting a preference, they were contradicting their own liberal views on the unimportance of race and racial difference.

Furthermore, some participants were uncomfortable and felt rather hypocritical if they expressed a preference, even when they themselves were mixed race and their relationships with their partners were interracial. Believing that in principle they should have no problems with their children partnering with whomever they wanted, some nevertheless did have fairly strong views and feelings, which were not always easily articulated.

For instance, despite her sheepish disclaimers about it not being socially acceptable, Kate (Black/White, 35) spoke of her own partnerships and her aversion to dating White men because of her wish to retain the "Black line," a desire rooted in her knowledge about slavery and the strategic breeding between White and Black people to diminish the Black line. Such feelings also influenced how she felt about her children's partnerships:

> KATE: I'll see a mixed-race couple, and there's still part of me that feels *funny*, I don't know why . . . but it's like, "Kate, why can't you accept this, why is it not acceptable?"
>
> INT: Ok, do you mean mixed . . .
>
> KATE: In terms of Black and White. And I see them with their little kids, and even my brother who's got a White wife as well, and mixed-race children. . . . He's still up in [a northern town], they get some racism up there. So yeah, and I'm like "This is where you come from [Kate]! This situation is what created you," and I think, there was a part of me, and I think there are some mixed-race people that are the same way as well, where they want to continue the Black line . . . And so when I see it I still feel people are trying to stop the Black line. And I think, "This is surprising that this Black man is with a White woman, why does he have to be with a White woman?" And I feel like I fight with myself because I feel like it's politically incorrect for me to have those thoughts but there's part of me that feels funny. And so I try to be really smiley and just ignore it, and it's just . . . I could walk past a gay couple easier than I could a mixed-race couple.

Later in the interview, the conversation turned to her own children.

> INT: Thinking about . . . it's hard to say in the future, but have you got any preference for who you'd want your kids to partner with?
>
> KATE: No . . . (she pauses).
>
> INT: You can be as honest as you like . . .

KATE: I suppose, I wouldn't really care . . . but if they didn't have them [partners] with Black, mixed-race [people] I would feel about the line . . . but I think the whole line thing is because I learned so much about the rape of the slaves and maybe being mixed race was kind of . . . a strategy for decreasing the black population of the world, so it's almost like you're trying to . . . you'll find lots of people going back to Africa, even if they're from the Caribbean, finding their African names, getting their land in Africa, and it's almost like they're trying to get back what was stolen from them. And I think when it comes to having children, I mean, they're saying that by a certain year the world will be full of mixed-race people, because we're all so mixed . . . and I think lots can be said for music joining people together as well . . . but I think it's that if I analyze it . . . I suppose I would be *slightly disappointed.* (She laughs).

INT: That's ok . . .

KATE: It's weird, but I think that might be the case. I don't think it's acceptable to think like that, I think it's wrong, but I think it's . . . if it happened, then I'd just accept it, same as if they told me that they were gay or lesbian.

In this frank interview, Kate struggled with the fact that she is uncomfortable with Black/White interracial relationships (whereas she appeared not to be as bothered by other types of interracial relationships), even though she is the "product" of such a relationship herself. This unease is related to her knowledge of Black denigration and enslavement, historically, and an emotional connection with her Black line.

While other parents also articulated concerns about retaining an ethnic minority line, some were attracted to the idea of having a cosmopolitan, international partner for their children. For Diane (East Asian/White, 54), this meant someone who was not "just" White British:

DIANE: I don't see [my children] as fully White racially. . . . They've still got that . . . quarter Chinese.

INT: Is that quarter Chineseness something that you feel is important to pass down to your children or not?

DIANE: I think so . . . It does matter to me, yeah. . . . In fact . . . it's sad, the thought that it might get lost, you know. It would be quite nice if they . . . if their partners were mixed-race as well! (She laughs.) . . . It's just a thought, you know. It's not that important . . . obviously I want them to just be happy.

INT: Yeah. But you wouldn't mind if they partnered with someone with Chinese heritage?

DIANE: No, not at all. In fact, [her daughter] Rita, she's had two relationships, both with . . . someone from Brazil and then she's had . . . a relationship with a half-Turkish . . . And I suppose there's a bit of a sort of a tradition in my family . . . of different mixes—not racially necessarily—a tradition of being international. . . . I'd like it [her children to have mixed partnerships themselves] in lots of ways but having experienced, I guess, my parents and my husband, you know, not feeling at home in Britain, there's all sorts of challenges that it brings as well so I'd be, you know, wary of the . . . cautious of the challenges as well for, you know, wherever you are, one of you is not going to feel totally at home.

A number of participants who had a strong identification as multiracial were quite celebratory and excited about how their children would contribute to shaping the increasingly diverse world they inhabited through their own relationships with interesting others, who themselves could be mixed. For example, Cecilia (East Asian/White, 31) believed that her children were more likely to be understood by someone who was also mixed and that, in general, partners continuing to mix would foster more openness and diversity in the wider world.

INT: Would you have any preference for who [your children] might partner with in the future in terms of ethnicity or race?

CECILIA: Well, not really but it would be nice for the future of the world if they partner with somebody who is also mixed race. I think also it . . . will make them feel more understood, like their partner knows where they're coming from, but not any particular mix or anything.

Christian (East Asian/White, 53) articulated similar feelings about encouraging mixture, and, like Diane, he noted that it was part of a family tradition to mix. However, he also took what Chamion Caballero has called the "hybrid vigour" attitude toward mixing, that genetic mixing produced a hardy, genetically superior individual:[3]

INT: Do you have any sense or preference for who she [his daughter] might partner with in the future?
CHRISTIAN: No, it makes no difference at all . . . no. I'm trying to think who [in the family] would [have a preference]. The Chinese tend to like to stick with Chinese but our family is slightly different because so many of my father's siblings actually married outside the Chinese community. Indian, German . . . so they were a bit different anyway. So it's not so . . . traditional if you like.
INT: And based on your experience of growing up mixed and identifying as a mixed-race person, do you think you would advocate having mixed relationships or having children who end up being mixed race?
CHRISTIAN: Absolutely. Absolutely. . . . It follows along the lines of Darwin's theories of evolution, mixing is always good for the gene pool. Fact, end of story. Yeah. It adds to the richness of life, no?

Like Christian, Bina (South Asian/White, 47) actively celebrated the likelihood of her children's families being very mixed:

Whoever they choose, their kids [her children's children] will be mixed in any case, because they're not going to find somebody that's equal to who they are [that is, mixed in the same way as her children are], in terms of their own heritage. That is really unlikely. I doubt that, so they're going to meet somebody, whether they're English, French, Italian, or god knows what, so whatever happens it will be a mixture in any case, so their kids will be mixed. That's perfectly ok, I don't have a problem at all, I don't have any expectations, whatever will happen, will happen, and it will be fine. I will be very excited about it. The possibilities are endless! (She laughs.)

As Bina points out, her children are unlikely to encounter someone who is mixed in precisely the same way they are—namely, Indian/French/Japanese/White American (Bina's and her children's father's ancestries combined). So any partner would create a further "mix," opening up a multiplicity of possible ethnic combinations.

Concerns about "Dilution"

A celebratory and positive understanding of "mixing," especially down the generations, however, was also often tinged with sadness about the cultural loss of a minority heritage (as articulated by Diane, above) and concern with ethnic and racial "dilution." We were struck by how prevalent this theme was among our participants. Even though many participants noted the socially constructed and problematic nature of race and racial difference, those who had White partners in particular frequently drew on notions of blood quantum and the idea of ethnic and racial dilution, especially in relation to their children.

For many participants in this study, these concerns could be triggered by the death of a minority parent and the sense that that minority heritage would be difficult to sustain. As Hari (South Asian/White, 29) put it:

I think also, because my partner is White English and I suppose also, given, you know, my dad died. . . . I don't really have very much contact with his [Indian] family. I do have some contact but not as much as when we were growing up. I suppose sometimes I do feel a bit of loss, part of me that is perhaps not missing, but I suppose that's a difference that I do feel a bit. Whereas growing up I did feel that I had very much a dual identity because we did used to go to weddings and things with my dad's family.

A related question we asked our participants was whether they thought ethnic and racial dilution (in terms of lineage) was inevitable, especially in terms of their children's choice of partner. Of the many participants who had White partners (46 of 62), Drew's (South Asian/White, 47) thoughts about his Indian ancestry and his children were quite typical:

They're proud of being a quarter Indian but, if . . . one of them or both of them don't marry somebody who's either mixed race or of another race then, you know, it'll be a sort of happy memory of dad and granddad sort of thing.

Drew's belief that his Indian heritage is not likely to be sustained or revitalized was related, in part, to the fact that he and his family lived in a mostly White city in the South East where most of his wider social network was White. Nevertheless, Drew valued his Indian connections, and he made occasional visits to India with his wife and children to see his relatives. If he expressed a tinge of sadness, he was mainly philosophical about his children's future partners as well as the inevitable loss or forgetting of family history and lineage over time (not uncommon in families more generally). This excerpt also reflects his refusal to put too much store upon ethnicity per se.

In comparison with Drew, Rose (East Asian/White, 45) was very sad about her Chinese heritage ebbing away. While Rose had dark hair and eyes and was usually seen as racially ambiguous (but was sometimes seen as "Chinese"—the dominant ethnicity of many British people associated with an East Asian ancestry), her children looked completely White, and this could be rather unsettling for her:

INT: Do you think that becoming a parent in any way changed your . . .
thinking about yourself or the significance of your ethnic and racial
background?

ROSE: Well, I suppose there was the question of what will my children
look like? And both my children came out blonde with blue eyes and
I was completely stunned! (She laughs.) It wasn't what I was expecting . . . wasn't what I was expecting at all because I mean my eyes
aren't particularly dark but my brother certainly has got very dark
eyes. My brother's darker than me but we both, you know, have got
dark hair and darkish eyes.

INT: So you were surprised?

ROSE: I was really surprised and I felt a bit disappointed because . . .
it felt like it was an erasure of part of my own heritage. . . . I did
feel that on a sort of biological erasure of . . . of . . . of me on some
level . . .

At the time of the interview, Rose's father (who had lived in China) had
recently died, and she spoke about her sense of the tenuousness of her
ties with her Chinese ancestry with great sadness. And her children's
blonde hair and blue eyes were a reminder of her (and their) fragile connection with her Chinese side of the family.

However, not all respondents who spoke of ethnic dilution felt sad
about it, particularly if they had very little connection with their minority heritage whether in terms of distinctive cultural practices or ties
with relatives. Kevin (South Asian/White, 39) had been raised in foster
care, and had had little exposure to his Bangladeshi father's heritage. He
was now married to a White English woman, and he spoke of his sense
of distance from his Bangladeshi background throughout his interview
and his belief that his children's connection with their Bangladeshi background would be even more tenuous:

Speaking truthfully, I don't think it [his Bangladeshi ancestry] would be
a significant part of their lives. . . . And I think probably I'm a good ex-

ample of how, to use the phrase, "dilution," how it kind of . . . . it's not to be without identity, but I think the boys will have the same thing, I think they'll just grow up . . . of the feeling, not of the opinion but of the feeling, that they're predominantly White, that's it. And so in that regard I think over time, there will be a loss of some things.

For Kevin, his Bangladeshi heritage was not that salient to him or to his day-to-day life, and he assumed that it would be of even less relevance to his children. Here, Kevin demonstrates a very matter of fact attitude about the inevitability of "dilution," rather than an emphasis on an irrevocable loss which is laden with emotions and meanings.

Yet an acknowledgement and discussion of dilution did not necessarily mean that cultural practices or identities would be affected—especially for those with some Black ancestry. Some participants, including some second-generation mixed people such as James (Black/White, 43) claimed strong minority identifications, in spite of (or because of) their generational remove:

INT: I wanted to quickly ask you . . . I'm curious, I mean your mum is
    mixed [Black Caribbean and White English] herself, and if one can
    put it this way, you're one generation removed. Do you think that's at
    all meaningful, I mean do you think that matters at all?
JAMES: Yeah, I think it's significant because I think it was probably
    tougher in that era for my mum. . . . It wasn't *not* tough for us but
    it was a lot tougher for, you know the eldest of twelve kids moved
    around and you can pretty much guarantee they moved around so
    much because of the racial abuse I'm going to guess. Nobody's actu-
    ally said that but it's pretty clear that it would be that . . . until they
    settled in [x]. But my [Black] identity's probably stronger than my
    mum's I would say.
INT: How interesting. What do you mean by that?
JAMES: In terms of my kind of understanding of history and the impact
    of it and the political ramifications. . . . I identify with the Black race,

with some of the experiences that people have had and I wouldn't
have got here and I'm certain people have had things done to them
throughout the years and you know that type of thing, you know,
certainly my mum's mum and dad, you know, they met in Liverpool
and then moved down, but they moved all the way through the
country and it was all the time and they had so many kids you have
to ask why they had so many kids. I'm going to guess it's about family
and about being accepted and other, other factors as well but all of
that, all of that has to play a part to it as well.

While James acknowledged that his mother had, in his words, "a higher
percentage," of Black ancestry than he did (his father was White), James
clearly felt a strong sense of Black identity, regardless of blood quantum
measures and generational remove. If anything, he was saying that he
was much more attached to his Blackness than his mother, who grew up
in a different time and place, where it was not common to affirm one's
Black heritage in a politicized way (at least not in her family, or in her
immediate surroundings). Therefore generational remove did not automatically mean further distancing from one's minority heritage for some
participants, although they were in the minority.

The Future of Racial Boundaries and Awareness in Britain
Feeling Commonality with Other Mixed People

Given the significant increase in mixed unions and mixed people of
various backgrounds, we asked our participants toward the end of our
interviews whether they felt any sense of connection or affiliation with
other multiracial people. In doing so, we wanted to explore if they perceived an emergent sense of mixed people constituting a group as such.[4]

In the United States, a 2015 Pew survey found little evidence of a
shared sense of commonality: Only about one third of those surveyed
believed they had a lot in common with other multiracials of the same
racial mix as they, while even less (17 percent) felt a sense of commonal-

ity with other multiracials of different racial backgrounds. However, the survey also found that "when they do wed, mixed-race Americans are more likely than other adults to marry someone who also is multiracial. Mixed-race adults are also more likely than the general public to have close friends or neighbors who are multiracial."[5]

By comparison, 28 of the 62 participants in this much smaller British study reported that they identified with mixed people *in general*, while 6 reported that they identified only with people of the same "mix" as themselves, and just under half the participants (28) reported that they felt no automatic commonality with other mixed people. The bases for some reported sense of commonality or identification with other mixed people varied. For some, it crystallized around the theme of cultural and ethnic in-between-ness. In addition, a related theme of marginality was quite prominent in some interviews, and while this sense of marginality evoked a negative sense of not fully belonging to existing categories or groups, it also manifest itself in terms of a sense of commonality with other multiracial people, as in the case of Diane (East Asian/White, 54):

> I do feel . . . I do definitely feel a link. That's one of the things about being mixed race is that you never feel you totally belong to either. . . . I'm sometimes aware of being different. Sometimes people will see that I look a bit different so ask me about it. And then, as I say, when I meet Chinese people, I don't feel totally the same as . . . and I don't feel I belong so. . . . Yes, so sometimes you can feel well, I'm not either. I'm not anything really.

Sophie (Black/White, 31), also felt a broad sense of commonality with other mixed people:

> All the mixed race people you meet, you will have certain things that you get from one of your parents and then the other, but you don't have a natural . . . like you can't say, "Oh, you're Spanish, this is how you do things," so you don't really have that. So as I've got older I tend to . . . I'm more drawn to mixed race people . . . because they understand.

In comparison with East Asian/White and South Asian/White participants, more than half (22 of 32) of Black/White participants claimed to identify either with other mixed people generally or with other Black/White mixed people specifically. While the small and unequal number of South Asian/White and East Asian/White respondents makes a direct comparison with Black/White respondents difficult, it was the case that fewer South Asian/White (8 of 19) and (4 of 11) East Asian/White respondents reported a sense of commonality with mixed people generally (or with those who shared their Asian ancestries). This may suggest the emergence of a specifically Black/White sense of multiraciality in Britain, which is not as evident among other types of mixed people. However, just under a third of Black/White participants reported no sense of commonality with other mixed people, as in Stephen's (Black/White, 27) case:

The reason I would say no would be because [of] . . . the variety of people's journeys, and experience of mixed race. . . . You don't automatically have an affinity with anyone. [So] to then go, "Oh, you're mixed race therefore you must be roughly similar to me" doesn't quite tie in.

For a small number of participants, claiming and celebrating a multiracial identity had practical implications in their social lives in that they made a concerted effort to meet and socialize with other mixed people in Britain, both online and in person. For instance, when asked if he felt a sense of commonality with other mixed people, Laheem (Black/White, 45) replied:

Yes, it's like what I told some new friends through a meet-up in London, in a pub. I'm on a healing mission—I don't know about you guys, but I want to explore, via these conversations, to find people of like minds and like hearts. But I'm finding some amazing stories, but also some sad stories.

While some, like Laheem, felt a distinctive bond with other multiracial individuals, many participants (regardless of the strength of their connection with other mixed people) stressed that they, and multiracial people more generally, were, in fact, entirely normal. As Tara (Black/White, 50) put it:

> I mean, I think most important for me, is to have mixedness normalized. I hate the way it's like the people are either bigging it up, "Oh, it's a great thing, a great thing!," or putting it down. It is just a normal experience. And it's very difficult trying to make changes in that because you always get people up from one end of the spectrum or the other. . . . But, . . . you know, we are the middle ground, that's where, you know, we live, really.

Transcending Race and Emphasizing Cosmopolitanism

We also asked our participants about what they thought would happen with ethnic and racial boundaries and awareness in the future. While they realized that it was difficult to discern exactly how the increase in the numbers of multiracial people (and their children) would shape these dynamics, they had little doubt that this increase did in itself signal a major sea change. Insofar as they did speculate, though, most participants envisioned a mixed scenario, in which ethnic and racial boundaries would grow weaker, while various forms of racial awareness, gate-keeping, and prejudice would continue. They also noted that forms of "othering" were not necessarily racial as such and could involve xenophobic attitudes as well. Either way, the majority of participants were cautiously optimistic about how "mixing" would impact the wider society. Ingrid (Black/White, 44) put it this way:

> I kind of think maybe the way people talk about race, which has up until now been "Black/White," I think that might start to change as there's more and more people. . . . Because in my generation in Britain, we were just a very small, it feels like, we were a very small group. But that's going to change, because there's going to be so many more people, and so many more mixed relationships, that there might be more of a sense of a third

category than there's been up until now. So I'm not sure what that will do, but I think it will be significant. . . . So . . . it'll just be interesting to see, but certainly that rise in the number of people from mixed parentage, it'll just be really interesting to see those numbers grow, and see that as more of a group.

Like Ingrid, many of our participants believed that being mixed (in a variety of ways) would increasingly be the norm. Ingrid also believed that the pace of social change, along with the increase in numbers of mixed people and relationships, would lead to a less binary understanding of ethnic and racial difference:

This binary idea is kind of "Black/White" and it's actually quite difficult, it's breaking down anyway, so . . . um, and say in an area like this, you're going to get, it's not going to just be people from African or Caribbean mixing with white people. It's going to be Asian people, Turkish people, it's going to be so much more in the pot, so ideally you might get to a stage where that's seen as the norm, that there isn't just the idea of this pure White English, which is kind of bogus anyway, when you think about all the different, if you go back far enough and all the different people that have come into these isles and influenced them, so it might be that over time, certainly in the cities that . . . that the idea of Britishness will just embrace all of that really. That will be what you could hope for.

Regardless of what they thought would happen, many participants similarly articulated such a hope that British society would transcend rigid notions of race and racial difference. For instance, Bina celebrated the idea of multiraciality in terms of "crossing over":

It's something that a lot of people think about, what is the answer to the future, to a lot of problems that we're facing, and it is about this crossing over, because the more you cross over, then the more you're not hanging on to what actually divides people or separates people. I see them as part of that new . . . generation which you know, let's say will take over the world one day, and there's a long way to go because there are so many countries where intermarriage are [sic] frowned upon and not allowed. So it still takes a lot of guts and courage for people to do it in certain parts of the world. Whereas now, here, it doesn't. I think here it's completely acceptable and normal, and ok.

Those, like Bina, who were quite optimistic about the possibility of mixed people being at the vanguard of a newly emergent sensibility in which traditional understandings of differences simply ceased to matter, emphasized a cosmopolitan sense of belonging in the world. As Bina said,

This is my opinion, I might get it completely wrong, but that's from conversations that I've had with them [her children], or what they share with me. . . . I've often described myself as a citizen of the world, and this is what I've passed on to them as well, it's like, when you have so many variations, the sense of belonging . . . what do you actually belong to? Well, you belong to humanity, you belong to . . . it becomes bigger, and we're not limiting it, and building boundaries to define who you are.

For Tanya (Black/White, 34), the growth of mixed families such as her own was indicative of growing societal acceptance of "difference," and she drew a parallel between her mixed family and the status of gay couples and families:

And maybe that's really wishful thinking on my part, but I think unconsciously, the way that as a family I think we probably have high levels of acceptance around others who are different. And we value inclusivity. There's a warmth towards others who are outsiders, whether that be gay couples who are raising children, like our neighbors who are gay, or other families who are poorer, I don't know. I just think in that way there's an empathy.

This coupling of ethnic and racial acceptance with acceptance of and warmth toward other people who have historically been "outsiders," such as gay people, suggests that there may be some level of empathy or affiliation or connection with those others who have been discriminated against by the white, heterosexual mainstream and that among those who have been "othered" in various ways some sense of solidarity can emerge.

Not all participants, however, were this sanguine. Laila (South Asian/White, 42) was especially concerned about the current criticism of multicultural discourse in Britain and on the European continent:

> You've got a good mixing part growing already, but I think you'll still have communities that want to stay distinctive and separate. I think you get that quite clearly, especially in the current environment, I think, especially with the end of, you know, that kind of . . . the policy . . . the policy emphasis on multiculturalism and how that's shifted now yet again, you know, to integration and the implications of all of that, I think, are going to be quite big.

Even before "Brexit" (the referendum for Britain to leave the European Union, held in June 2016) and the controversial election of Donald Trump, some participants expressed concerns about the contemporary political climate. Like Laila, Gina (Black/White, 44) mentioned being troubled by the growing popularity of the United Kingdom Independence Party (UKIP) and its anti-immigration platform.

> Um . . . I kind of worry sometimes . . . well, you know you've got UKIP now that are strong in the country, and that always makes me sad because there are that many people who seem to feel . . . it's not that they hate people who are not white, but that's kind of the message coming across. And there's so much about anti-immigration and all this, and I always feel a bit like, "Well, my family came from immigrants, and there's a lot of people like me," that I feel are . . . well, it hurts your feelings a bit when you're British, and that's going on. So that side worries me a bit, UKIP,

and I would hope that people do just become tolerant, really tolerant of all the races, because to me, Britain is multicultural, it is a multicultural country, that's what it is now.

As a number of participants observed, the increasing numbers of mixed relationships and mixed people, and the blurring of racial divides associated with those trends, did not preclude the formation or persistence of other kinds of racial and xenophobic discourses. Regardless of their specific ethnic and racial "mix," many of our participants had a heightened awareness of how British people of South Asian origin who were Muslim were regarded as a particularly feared "other." Furthermore, in light of various racist and xenophobic incidents reported since the recent referendum to leave the European Union, such concerns appear quite justified.[6]

Conclusion

In the aftermath of the controversy (and fatwa) surrounding *The Satanic Verses*, Salman Rushdie defended and celebrated "hybridity, impurity, intermingling, the transformation that comes of new and unexpected combinations of human beings."[7] Much of Rushdie's work has both celebrated the products of translation and mixture (mélange) and addressed what Stuart Hall calls the "oscillation between Tradition and Translation."[8] For my part, I was struck by how many participants drew upon similar notions of hybridity and translation in talking about multiracial people and their children. That is, many of the multiracial participants in this study talked of their children as being, in effect, in translation, or as drawing upon various cultural and ethnic traditions.[9] At the same time, many parents still subscribed to notions of roots and felt strongly about cultural and ethnic traditions and practices that were subject to irrevocable loss. On the whole, though, our participants were relatively optimistic that the increase in mixed relationships and people and their increasing commonality through much of Britain signaled a general lessening of racial divides—although they also recognized that the pace of change was greater in urban areas than in suburban and semirural areas, which were much more White. Many participants adopted a generational perspective in thinking about the future, and what was in store for their children. In comparison with their own childhoods, and the experiences of their parents in what had been a much more ethnically homogeneous and racially hostile environment, all of our participants acknowledged how much had changed, for the better—though here, too, such an understanding was tempered by the awareness that prejudicial thinking and xenophobic attitudes and discourses were not just a remnant of the past.

Despite our participants' appreciation for the fact that ethnic and racial denigration and openly discriminatory treatment was no longer tolerated, many also expressed a degree of ambivalence about some of the implications of more blurred racial boundaries and social "integration." For instance, many of our participants (most of whom had had children with White partners) were concerned with ethnic and racial "dilution," especially in terms of their children's choice of partners and what this could mean for their children's children. While the majority of participants reported that they had no preference regarding the ethnic and racial backgrounds of their children's future partners, a small number of participants did have strong views. Moreover, among those who were reluctant to state one way or another, some did eventually reveal that they harbored particular preferences, and of these, many spoke of their wish that their children would partner with someone who shared their minority ancestry or with someone who was not White. In particular, some of the Black/White participants expressed discomfort with the possibility that their children might have White partners—even when these participants themselves had had White parents or partners.

Some participants who believed that their children would most likely partner with White Britons saw "dilution" as being inevitable. Others, however, who had partnered with other mixed or co-ethnic minority individuals saw their children as potentially revitalizing a minority heritage or contributing to a "melting pot" scenario in which clearly demarcated ethnic and racial backgrounds would become less and less common.

Moreover, while there was a consensus that significant demographic and normative changes were occurring, in which mixed people and unions were increasingly common, most people who reported a sense of shared experience with other mixed people articulated this rather tentatively, noting the many disparate aspects of people's backgrounds and life experiences that militated against an easy recognition of "the" multiracial population in Britain. At the same time, however, many participants of all ethnic and racial backgrounds agreed that being mixed would be wholly "normal" in the coming generation or two. Louise (Black/White, 44), for one, believed that while her son Jake (22) still had to explain his mixedness to others (though in much less hostile circumstances than when she was growing up), this would no longer be the case in the future:

> He [Jake] certainly isn't unusual. So it's probably very, very normal, and I think for the generation that comes after him, it will be like it's always been. So I think that will be . . . the public face of mixed-race Britain is more and more prevalent, it's everywhere now, in all walks of life . . . I think Intermix [a website] will cease to be relevant to my son's children's generation, the idea that you would need to go somewhere to talk to other people in a forum about being mixed race . . . it will seem so anachronistic to them, they just won't need it. It'll be like going to a forum with other people who are five foot three and a half. And I think in the census, mixed race is the largest growing? It'll just be "whatever," or one day it might be "What, both your parents are Black . . . or White!? That's weird mate. I couldn't hack that." . . . And for him [Jake], it isn't background noise because he still has to justify how he looks, and how he got to be that way. But I think for his children or his children's children, it will be background noise.

Conclusion

A Generational Tipping Point

This book has broken new ground, as it is the first to investigate the experiences of multiracial people who are parents (as opposed to parents in interracial unions) and the ways in which they identify and raise their children. By focusing specifically on multiracial people and their children, we have been able to explore the meanings and practices around multiracial status down a generation, including the continuing salience (or not) of ethnic and racial identification (or an attachment to the idea of being mixed per se).

This study has extended quantitative studies of how interracial couples in the United States racially identify their multiracial children. I have argued that we cannot simply "read off" the racial labels that parents apply to their multiracial children. These designations require unpacking and interpretation—they do not speak for themselves. As this book has shown, what it means for parents to designate their children as "mixed" or "White" can be variable and be motivated by a number of concerns—and not just an instrumental decision about buying into White privilege.

A focus upon multiracial parents has shown that they face choices, and often uncertainty, about how they should identify their children, and that there are no clear conventions for doing so. However, it is striking that so many of the participants (including Black/White participants and even some participants with children who looked White) did identify their children as mixed.[1] Even Black/White participants with Black partners in this study reported that they would identify their children as "mixed" (and indeed, *saw* them as mixed)—in contrast with findings in the United States, where such a classification by a Black/White and Black couple was much less likely.[2]

Furthermore, the ways in which parents racially identify their children on official forms (such as a decennial census) may not correspond in any straightforward way with how they are actually raising them. For example, most of the participants who raised their children with an emphasis upon a minority ancestry identified their children as "mixed," thus suggesting that the identification of children as "mixed" did not necessarily signal a distancing from one's minority ancestry. Moreover, some of the participants who reported that they identified their children as White (though such participants were in the minority) still reported raising them with an emphasis on cosmopolitan ideals and practices, as opposed to raising them as "just" British. In fact, the majority of participants in this study reported a cosmopolitan upbringing for their children, and they wanted their children to live in a world that was ethnically diverse and culturally hybrid. The valuing of cosmopolitanism by many of the participants tended to draw upon a wider discourse of inclusion and "otherness," in which being multiracial (as opposed to a monoracial designation) was increasingly normal and only one way in which the wider society was diversifying (others included gay couples, for example, and alternative lifestyles). In this context, a number of mixed participants saw themselves and their families as constituting the vanguard of a diverse and more inclusive Britain.

The Ethnic Options of Multiracial People and Their Children

Various scholars in the United States have argued that, on the whole, the one-drop rule of hypodescent is declining in significance.[3] Many of the *first-generation* multiracial participants in this study, especially the Black/White participants, and some East Asian/White and South Asian/White participants, were identified as monoracial minorities or as racially ambiguous non-White others. However, down a generation, where many of the first-generation participants had children who looked White and whose ancestry was mostly White, the rule of hypodescent rarely applied to their children.[4] In the case of the small number of *second-generation* multiracial participants in this study, those with White partners had third-generation children who were seen as unambiguously White. By comparison, the experiences of both first- and second-generation participants who had *non-White* partners could suggest a revitalization of the rule of hypodescent, since their children looked non-White to others.

For the children of some first-generation participants (usually South Asian/White and East Asian/White) with White partners and for those of most (though not all) second-generation participants with White partners, their minority ancestry was typically invisible to others. Consequently, theirs was becoming an increasingly symbolic ethnicity unless they made a concerted effort to work at reanimating specific aspects of their mixedness. However, it would be erroneous to conclude that a straightforward whitening among multiracial people and their children is irrevocable. Despite some exceptions, most participants in this study still designated their children as "mixed," even when their children appeared White to others. This tendency suggests that in Britain a mixed identification is gaining purchase, even for the second-generation children of multiracial individuals.

Although many participants insisted upon their children being identified as "mixed," they understood that their assertions were not necessarily validated by others. Interestingly, *uncertainty was pronounced for those participants with White partners*, especially if those participants felt that their minority ancestry was simply too far removed from the day-to-day lives of their children. By comparison, *those with minority partners (with whom they did or did not share racial ancestry)* did not report as much uncertainty per se.

The physical appearance of children was often fundamental in this regard. Those participants with children who did not appear White to others (and this could include looking racially ambiguous) did not designate their children as White (they were categorized as mixed), but some parents whose children *did* look White to others could experience uncertainty (and in some cases, trepidation) about whether they were "allowed" to describe their children as multiracial or mixed.

While many of our relatively educated participants noted that race was a social construction and denied the biological or genetic basis of race and racial difference (and implied that to do so was somehow inherently racist and reproduced benighted notions of racial difference), they often slipped into a discussion of the significance of blood quantums and racial fractions in explaining how they identified their children.[5] For instance, some participants felt unable to justify the assertion of a "mixed" label for their children on the grounds that while they themselves were "fifty/fifty," their own children were typically only "a quarter" minority, which in turn, translated into their uncertainty about being able to justify a mixed identification for their children.

On the other hand, some participants not only knowingly defied fractional understandings of who is and is not mixed, but also denied that one's physical appearance (as White) precluded a legitimate assertion of a mixed identity and status. Is it possible that a multigeneration mixed identity is emergent, one that is *not* dependent upon the "proof" of a non-White physical appearance? The fact that many first-generation (and some second-generation) multiracial participants claimed that their children, too, were mixed, is also a way of asserting the genealogical connectedness between multiracial parents and their children, especially in cases where multiracial parents who don't look White have White-looking children. Only time will tell if the children designated as mixed by their multiracial parents will embrace such identities themselves.

How Distinctive Are the Experiences of Black/White People in Britain?

Studies in the United States suggest the continuing importance of racial classifications by others made on the basis of appearance and distinctive racial phenotypes. In fact, Cynthia Feliciano argues that a "dark-skin rule" (of racially assigning someone who is visibly dark skinned) is now typically more significant than the one-drop rule (especially if someone with a small amount of Black ancestry does not look Black).[6] Even as being multiracial becomes ever more ordinary, the idea of a broad multiracial identity is still inchoate and contested. While some analysts conceive of mixedness as a shared experience and identity, transcending the specifics of particular groups, others are much more skeptical about the purported commonalities among, say, Black/White mixed people and East Asian/White people.[7]

As discussed in prior chapters, there is some evidence for the idea of Black exceptionalism in relation to multiracial people with Black ancestry in Britain; however, the experiences of part-Black people in Britain are also distinctive from those of part-Black people and African Americans in the United States.[8] Some scholars have argued that in the United States Black (or part-Black) people differ markedly from their Asian and Latino counterparts in that they are less likely to intermarry with White people. They also note that Black/White multiracial people in the United States are less likely to identify as multiracial (and more likely to identify as Black),[9] in large part because other Americans see them as Black, given the indelible history of slavery and its aftermath, as opposed to the voluntary immigration histories of most Asian and Latino Americans.[10]

However, as shown in Jenifer Bratter's research (see chapter 2), there is likely to be more flux and variation in the identifications and experiences of Black and part-Black people than is acknowledged in some writings. A recognition of the growing salience of different multiracial identifications and groups (including part-Black multiracials) need not (and should not) be automatically assumed to legitimize the idea of a post-racial society. There needs to be more investigation of how different types of multiracial people think about and value disparate aspects of their ethnic and racial ancestries, as analyses that still rely upon the traditional binary of White and Black may obscure other racial formations. For instance, Carolyn Liebler finds that in the last half century in the United States, part-White people have been *decreasingly* reported as monoracially White.[11] This finding is at odds with (or at least complicates) the claim made by some analysts that Asian/White multiracials are increasingly part of the White fold in American society.

Unlike Black and Black/White people in the United States, Black and Black/White people in Britain have much higher rates of intermarriage with White Britons, and many Black/White people in Britain embrace the label "mixed."[12] On the whole, the Black/White participants (who comprised the largest number of mixed people in the sample) reported a stronger awareness of potential forms of racism, a greater collective consciousness of a Black history and experience that has been marked by racial denigration and disadvantage, and an emergent sense of a Black/White multiracial identity and experience.[13] It is important to note that for many of our Black/White participants, this racial awareness was also linked to a positive sense of Blackness and Black history, which they recognized was not readily available for many British people of South Asian or East Asian backgrounds, given the predominantly negative depictions of South Asian Muslims and the social invisibility of Chinese- and Vietnamese-origin Britons.[14]. By comparison, many of these Black/White participants, and especially those in urban centers, saw themselves as accepted members of the British mainstream.[15]

In some urban regions, there was evidence of generationally embedded social networks of Black/White multiracial people, many of whom had multiracial parents, relatives, and friends.[16] This sense of a shared collective experience, as Black *and* White mixed, was not found among East Asian/White or South Asian/White participants, who appear to have been more geographically atomized. Furthermore, many of the White spouses of Black/White participants showed themselves to have a heightened sense of racial awareness. Such White spouses may already have been more racially conscious than many other White people, even prior to their unions with their part-Black partners, but it is also possible that their relationships with their Black/White partners enhanced their awareness of racial concerns and continuing forms of racism.

However, it is important not to homogenize the experiences and perceptions of part- Black people in this study or to generalize about them in British society more widely. Despite the fact that this subgroup was particularly racially conscious and attune to the importance of fostering racial awareness in their children, we should not assume that part-Black people relate to both the Black and White worlds in the same ways. For instance, some Black/White participants in this study reported that they did not feel culturally or socially Black, especially if they had grown up in predominantly White settings and raised primarily by their White parent. Furthermore, many Black/White participants shared views about cosmopolitan norms and practices as parents—much like the other non-Black parents in this study.

Are Multiracial People Distancing Themselves from Minority Status?

Many US scholars argue that the dominant racial ideology in the United States in the post–Civil Rights period is color-blindness, which purports to transcend race and racial difference, but which effectively minimizes the salience of race and its detrimental effects.[17] A key limitation to such debates in the United States, however, is that it has been framed primarily according to a binary of Black and White Americans. In the United States, few studies of interracial unions and multiracial people have yet to investigate other types of "mixing".[18]

The fact that most mixed people in Britain (of all racial backgrounds) currently partner with White individuals is undoubtedly significant. However, it is important not to overstate the process of "whitening" in Britain—at least in terms of how such multiracial people identify and raise their children. Rather, as demonstrated in this book, having a White partner did not automatically signal a homogeneous set of experiences, attitudes, and practices for these parents and their children.

Many of the multiracial participants in this study articulated beliefs, ideas, and aspirations that suggested that race should not be important, or that race should be transcended. At the same time, many of these same participants seemed uneasy about relinquishing a claim to racial and ethnic difference and expressed an emotional attachment to their minority selves and ancestries.[19] Given such ambivalence and tension, it would be reductionist to conclude that their embrace of multiracial identity and cosmopolitan ideals is an attempt to distance themselves from the stigma of being a racially marked minority. Many participants of all mixed backgrounds—Black/White, South Asian/White, East Asian/White—spoke all too knowingly about the privileges that accrued to a White phenotype and how children with a Black or racially ambiguous (non-White) appearance or an identifiably "foreign" name could be vulnerable to racial prejudices and mistreatment. But this recognition of White privilege did not dissuade them from propagating a view about the need to transcend what they saw as rigid modes of racial thinking.

A number of recent studies in the United States have suggested that multiracial people may take the opportunity to "whiten" themselves when they can. For instance, Aliya Saperstein and Andrew Penner found that an individual's race can change over time, and that some Americans whose social positions are elevated are "whitened" as a result and that others who experience downward social mobility find themselves "darkened."[20] In a similar vein, Vanatta Ford has warned against "plasticity" and the possibility of "multiracial aspirationalism" in which the claim to being multiracial can be an effort to distance oneself from the stigma of Blackness and thus be a form of anti-Black racism.[21] She (like various other scholars) also points out that only some people have physiognomies that give them real ethnic and racial options.

However, not all scholars of race interpret the designation of a multiracial identity as an attempt to whiten themselves. Paul Spickard points out that many historical figures—W. E. B. Du Bois among them—changed their racial identities over the course of their lives, and not necessarily in the direction of Whiteness.[22] It is possible that racial classification will gradually become more malleable; in both Britain and the United States it is certainly contested.[23] Since the whole apparatus of racial classification in virtually all North American and European societies has rested upon the idea that individuals can be categorized in an array of monoracial categories, the very fact of mixing seriously destabilizes such systems.[24] Spickard has also argued that rather than focusing solely on people who try to "pass" as White, scholars should also look at "shape shifting," or the wider range of ways in which people may wish to identify and to affiliate themselves in relation to a multitude of ethnic and racial groups, including some with which they share no ethnic and racial ancestry.[25]

For instance, Tomas Jimenez has pointed to the emergence of "affiliative ethnic identity"—"an individual identity rooted in knowledge, regular consumption and deployment of an ethnic culture that is unconnected to an individual's ethnic ancestry."[26] A number of institutional and demographic changes, he argues, have "elasticized the link between ancestry and culture," making the formation of affiliative ethnic identity possible.[27] The Rachel Dolezal controversy in the United States and the ensuing debates about long-established categories such as "Black" and the politics of ethnic minority group membership, have led analysts such as Rogers Brubaker to argue that "as basic categorical frameworks have become the objects of self-conscious debate, critical scrutiny, strategic choice, and political claims-making, they have lost their self-evidence, naturalness, and taken-for-grantedness.'[28]

It is undoubtedly the case that *some* multiracial people with Black and other minority backgrounds may wish to distance themselves from their minority ancestries due to concerns about racial stigma. However, as found in this book, the extent to which both first- and second-generation multiracial people who designate their own children as mixed suggests the opposite inclination: *rather than trying to distance themselves from minority ancestry, such multiracial people are trying to maintain and/or revitalize it.* In fact, many participants in this study expressed a sense of sadness and concern about ethnic and racial "dilution," and they wondered how they might retain some sort of meaningful link with a minority heritage, especially when they had children with White partners. Furthermore, some first- and second-generation participants made a concerted decision to partner with other (monoracial minority or multiracial) people.

The growing popularity of tracing family genealogies is notable in Britain, and as "mixing" becomes ever more widespread, this fascination with identifying ethnic and racial lineages is unlikely to abate in the near future. Many consumers of genetic ancestry tests in the United States have been African Americans, whose African ancestry was largely unknown. For them, such DNA tests have provided what Alondra Nelson has called a more concrete and "usable past."[29] In the case of multiracial people, it will be interesting to see which parts of their ethnic and racial ancestries will figure in their narratives and those of their descendants in the next few generations.

Most theories of ethnic change have tended to forecast gradual shifts from minority status to acceptance within the dominant majority (White) group.[30] However, in her studies of Native Indian ethnic renewal, Joanne Nagel has observed that "in a kind of 'reverse cultural transmission' the passing on of family history and tradition to one's offspring can prompt a nonethnically identified parent to learn about his or her ethnic ancestry and to take on a new ethnic self-awareness."[31] Compared to Native American peoples (and despite the large number of tribes), multiracial people in Britain do not comprise an ethnically distinctive and coherent group, but their situation does give rise to some interesting questions about the possibility of ethnic renewal.[32] It is possible that the children of some first-generation or even second-generation multiracial people will reverse the seemingly inevitable trend toward "dilution" by choosing non-White partners (with whom they may or may not share ethnic and racial ancestry). In various urban centers in Britain, the social networks of many young people are highly ethnically and racially diverse, and as discussed throughout this book, for them, being mixed is increasingly unremarkable. What we are seeing as families in Britain become increasingly mixed (and such mixing can occur at disparate generational loci) is in effect a process of ethnogenesis.

However, countering ethnic and racial "dilution" will not be easy. We may overestimate how much multiracial people actually know (and care) about their parental ancestries. Typically, this knowledge is quite limited to a few generations back (if that), and it may be remembered or passed down quite selectively.[33] In fact, according to a 2015 Pew survey, "Multiracial identity fades quickly with the generations. Among those whose ties to a mixed racial background come from a great-grandparent or older ancestor, only 13% consider themselves to be multiracial"[34]— whereas twice as many did so for a grandparent with a mixed racial background. With each generation, then, there is a kind of halving of multiracial identification, despite some exceptions to this trend.

One further consideration merits discussion: in addition to generational change, there is much scope for variation in how individual members of families think about, identify, and live their lives, as mixed people. For example, in an earlier study of mixed young people in Britain, I specifically examined the ways in which mixed *siblings'* identifications and experiences could differ, given that their racial appearances could vary—sometimes quite considerably.[35] Just as siblings within families may experience their racial selves quite differently, so, too, their individual friendships and choice of partners may diverge along ethnic and racial lines. Therefore, in addition to generational change, future studies of multiracial people need to look laterally, across the generations.

Specifying the Generational Locus of Mixture

In the future, the specific generational locus of mixture will be increasingly important in studies of multiracial people, as people will apply different standards about who and what "counts" as multiracial. Thus the meanings of "multiracial" and the determinants of who is and is not multiracial will continue to be in flux. As in the Pew survey of multiracial Americans, we, too, need to recognize that multiracial status spans several generations, not just one, and that the generational locus of this status can mean different things, depending on the individual.

For example, some participants in this study, such as Glen (second-generation Black/White), claimed that while his (first-generation Black/White) mother was mixed, he was not, because he had a White father and was a generation farther removed. On the other hand, another participant, Anna, who was also second-generation Black/White mixed and who also had a White father, *did* identify as a mixed person, but drew the line with her (third-generation) children. One could argue, here, that both Glen and Anna have identified a "tipping point" at which their multiracial ancestry is no longer salient or meaningful, either to them or their children. This tipping point can come from a loss of meaning and identification or it can arise from the sense that multiracial ancestry is simply not consequential for either the parent or his or her children—though the latter does not necessarily mean that one's multiracial ancestry is entirely devoid of meaning.

The generational tipping point at which one's multiracial ancestry becomes largely inconsequential, or purely symbolic, will differ across and within various types of mixed people. As in Britain as a whole, three quarters of the multiracial participants in this study had White (British/European/North American) partners. The findings in this book suggest that, in the case of multiracial people with White partners, the tipping point for part-Black people may be a generation farther down from that of many multiracial people with South Asian and East Asian ancestries. One key reason for this difference is that some second-generation Black people (that is, individuals with one Black grandparent) are still recognized, phenotypically, as Black, while it is relatively rare for other *second*-generation mixed South Asian or East Asian people to be racially assigned as non-White. Furthermore, as discussed above, the racial consciousness of participants with Black ancestry was generally more pronounced than in the case of other mixed people.

While only one quarter of the multiracial participants in this study had partners who were either multiracial themselves or single-race minority individuals, it is quite likely that, especially in diverse urban centers, multiracial people will increasingly partner with other non-White individuals, often with a racial overlap (as in the case of Black/White individuals partnered with either Black or Black/White individuals). As discussed in Chapter 1, the way in which the British Office for National Statistics measures "interethnic unions" is thus problematic because it tends to overlook racial overlap between multiracial people and their partners.[36]

If we telescope down another generation, to the case of second-generation multiracial people and the ways in which they see themselves *and* their children (and in this study, there were seven second-generation participants), the validity of census classifications such as "Mixed" (which do not specify the generational locus of mixture) is increasingly in question. As multigeneration mixedness grows, we need more reliable ways of measuring and recording data about people's ethnic and racial identifications and ancestries. Currently, hardly any studies (in either the United States or Britain) distinguish between known ancestry and identification by multiracial people, as the two do not always correspond.[37] We need to differentiate people who acknowledge a mixed heritage and ancestors, but who do not identify as multiracial as such, from those who do identify themselves (and possibly their children) as multiracial. It will also be important to distinguish between multiracial status (and identity) as denoting "more than one race" rather than "a race" per se[38]—as in the idea that being both Black and White constituted a distinctive race in itself, as articulated by some Black/White participants in this study.

Generational specificity concerning the locus of mixture will be a key methodological issue, too, for many forms of official data collection aim to capture the ethnic and racial diversity of a society. For example, the use of exact two-group categories in the census (for example, White and Asian), which suggests first-generation "mixedness" and which is the equivalent to "biracial" in the United States, cannot capture mixedness that is multigenerational (where one or both parents are mixed).[39] Nor can such two-group categories account for the fact that many multiracial people may identify in relation to more than two distinct categories.

Furthermore, most studies of intermarriage have not looked beyond the unions of monoracially different individuals.[40] Thus, given the changing demographics in which multiracial people loom large, understandings of intermarriage will have to address the issue of how multigeneration mixed people and their unions can be operationalized for future research.

Future Study

As the growth and normalization of mixed people (and their children) continues apace, more in-depth studies of how multiracial people, families, and communities, may differ, not only across ethnic mixes, but also by gender, as well as regional and class backgrounds, will be needed. Further investigation into how disparate types of multiracial people identify and raise their children will also be needed for a fuller understanding of the multiracial population and what this growing diversity bodes for racial fault lines. For instance, in addition to specifying the generational locus of mixture, we need to differentiate between multiracial people who have mostly White, as opposed to mostly non-White, ancestries. Despite a strong emphasis on cosmopolitanism among our parents, there is every indication that "mixed" people constitute a very heterogeneous sector of the population in terms of their social experiences, their racial and ethnic identifications, and the ways they bring up their children.

A key strength of this study has been that it has investigated different kinds of multiracial people and experiences (not just Black and White multiracial people). Increasingly, our understandings of racism and racial disadvantage in the twenty-first-century British context must recognize that various racialization processes are mutually constitutive of one another, and that they cannot easily be understood in relation to only one axis of privilege, disadvantage or valorization.[41] The emergence of multigeneration multiracials really demands that we look beyond Black and White meanings of "multiracial" and that we come to appreciate the varied understandings and experiences of what it means to be mixed.

However, this study has relied primarily upon an educated, middle-class sample, and future studies need to capture a more varied population that includes less privileged and less educated multiracial people and their children. Our participants were, on the whole, quite versed in various ideas and debates about race and racial difference. It may be that those of lower social class backgrounds are less able to choose and/or to assert their choices about how to identify their children.[42] Furthermore, while this study focuses specifically upon the views and experiences of multiracial individuals as parents, in the future it would be extremely valuable to consider the views of the other parent, whether he or she is White or non-White. Nevertheless, this book has provided new understandings of how and why multiracial parents identify and raise their children in the ways they do, and it has documented some of the major concerns that various multiracial people reported, whether in relation to their children and family lives, or in relation to the nature of ethnic and racial divides in the wider society.

More studies of mixed families outside of the US context can illuminate the historically and nationally specific contexts in which such families are increasingly becoming ordinary. While the studies from the United States have led the scholarship of mixed families, it is vital that we learn about multiracial people and their families in other societies. As the multiracial population diversifies both in terms of specific ethnic and racial ancestries and in terms of the generational locus of mixture, specific concepts and terms will emerge to delineate, and further refine, the diversity of mixed people, their children, and their grandchildren in many countries throughout the world.

APPENDIX

Participants

#	Name (pseud-onyms)	Gender	Age	Mixed ancestry of par-ticipant	No. of children	Ancestry of children's other parent	Occupation	Census region
1	Tara	Female	50	Black/White	2	White British	Office manager	London
2	Alice	Female	30	Black/White	2	White British	Accountant	London
3	Jane	Female	47	East Asian/White	3	White British	University lecturer/professor	South East
4	Christian	Male	53	East Asian/White	2	Greek Cypriot	Retired company director	London
5	Vanessa	Female	51	Black/White	3	Black Caribbean	Education welfare officer	London
6	Joanna	Female	57	Black/White	2	German	Director of documentary films	London
7	Jeff	Male	46	South Asian/White	2	White British	Manager in law firm	South East
8	Clare	Female	43	Black/White	2	White British	Mature student at arts college	London
9	Serena	Female	38	South Asian/White	2	White British	Preschool assistant	South East
10	Drew	Male	47	South Asian/White	2	White British	Secondary school teacher	South East
11	Amanda	Female	47	Black/White	3	White British	University lecturer/professor	South East

#	Name (pseud-onyms)	Gender	Age	Mixed ancestry of par-ticipant	No. of children	Ancestry of children's other parent	Occupation	Census region
12	Beverley	Female	43	East Asian/ White	2	White British	Parent/ homemaker	South East
13	Jonathon	Male	42	East Asian/ White	2	White British	University lecturer/ professor	South West
14	Josh	Male	32	South Asian/ White	2	Black African	Scientist	South East
15	Domi-nique	Female	47	East Asian/ White	1	White British	University lecturer/ professor	East Midlands
16	Anna	Female	44	2nd gen. Black/ White	2	White British	Director of a charity	South East
17	Jamila	Female	45	South Asian/ White	2	German	Textile designer	South East
18	Rose	Female	45	East Asian/ White	2	White British	University lecturer/ professor	South East
19	Lorna	Female	51	South Asian/ White	3	White British	Parent/ homemaker	South East
20	Brenda	Female	44	Black/ White	3	White British	Unemployed parent/ homemaker	South East
21	Aisha	Female	50	South Asian/ White	1	White British	Wine consultant	South East
22	Danielle	Female	26	Black/ White	1	Black African	Postgraduate student	London
23	Gemma	Female	32	Black/ White	1	Mixed Black/ White	School busi-ness manager	East Midlands
24	Joe	Male	49	Black/ White	3	German	University lecturer/ professor	London

#	Name (pseud-onyms)	Gender	Age	Mixed ancestry of par-ticipant	No. of children	Ancestry of children's other parent	Occupation	Census region
25	Glen	Male	41	2nd gen. Black/White	2	White British	Computer consultant	South East
26	Brian	Male	33	2nd gen. South Asian / White	2	Japanese	University administrator	South East
27	Cecilia	Female	31	East Asian/White	2	Italian	Company supplies manager	North West
28	Hari	Male	29	South Asian/White	1	White British	Scientist	East of England
29	Bina	Female	47	South Asian/White	2	Mixed Japa-nese/White American	Filmmaker	London
30	Matt	Male	50	South Asian/White	1	White British	Photographer	South East
31	Alberto	Male	39	South Asian/White	1	White British	Former banker, now a landlord	London
32	Claudia	Female	29	Black/White	1	White British	Charity worker	London
33	Elaine	Female	32	Black/White	3	White British	Govern-ment policy researcher for government	South East
34	Luke	Male	48	Black/White	4	White British	Teaching assistant for disabled children	South East
35	James	Male	43	2nd gen. Black/White	3	Danish	Social worker	West Midlands
36	Pauline	Female	55	East Asian/White	2	White British	Parent/homemaker	South East

#	Name (pseud-onyms)	Gender	Age	Mixed ancestry of par-ticipant	No. of children	Ancestry of children's other parent	Occupation	Census region
37	Gina	Female	32	Black/White	2	White British	Catering assistant	Scotland
38	Diane	Female	54	East Asian/White	2	White British	University lecturer/professor	South East
39	Malcolm	Male	26	2nd gen. Black/White	1	Mixed Black/White	Unemployed	North West
40	Elise	Female	44	Black/White	5	White British	University student	South East
41	Louise	Female	44	Black/White	1	Black British	Market researcher	London
42	Laila	Female	42	South Asian/White	2	Bengali	Director of a charity	South East
43	Ingrid	Female	44	Black/White	1	White British	Trade union official	London
44	Jeremy	Male	35	South Asian/White	2	White British	Homeless-ness outreach officer	London
45	Rachel	Female	51	South Asian/White	3	White British	Website development consultant	Wales
46	Nicole	Female	28	East Asian/White	1	White British	Primary school teacher	South East
47	Lenny	Male	40	2nd gen. Black/White	2	White British	Local council care services officer	North West
48	Dennis	Male	45	Black/White	5	Black British	Physical therapist	East Midlands
49	Rebecca	Female	51	Black/White	1	Mixed Black/White	Artist	London
50	Abike	Female	58	Black/White	3	White British	Teaching assistant for disabled children	London

#	Name (pseudonyms)	Gender	Age	Mixed ancestry of participant	No. of children	Ancestry of children's other parent	Occupation	Census region
51	Khalil	Male	62	South Asian/White	2	White British	University lecturer/professor	South East
52	Victor	Male	39	2nd gen. Black/White	1 (+ 1 stepson)	Black African	Shipping coordinator	North West
53	Edward	Male	33	East Asian/White	1	Black British	Drama teacher	London
54	Kevin	Male	39	South Asian/White	3	White British	Building surveyor	London
55	Kate	Female	35	Black/White	2	Mixed Jamaican/Indian/Scottish	Spanish teacher	London
56	Stephen	Male	27	Black/White	2	White British	Local authority manager	East of England
57	Sophie	Female	31	Black/White	1	Mixed Black/White	Civil servant	London
58	Laheem	Male	45	Black/White	1 (+ 1 stepson)	Mixed Native American & European	Call center worker	East of England
59	Evelyn	Female	43	South Asian/White	2	White British	Self-employed textile designer	South East
60	Tanya	Female	34	Black/White	3	White British	Parent/homemaker	London
61	Garrett	Male	50	Black/White	2	White North American	IT manager	London
62	Allan	Male	53	South Asian/White	3	Polish	Social worker	South East

NOTES

INTRODUCTION

1 Asthana and Smith 2009. More recently, there has been a flurry of media attention concerning Prince Harry's current relationship with the actress Meghan Markle, who is mixed race and described as a "glamorous brunette" and "not in the society blonde style of previous girlfriends" (Hirsch 2016, drawing on descriptions of Markle from the *Daily Mail*).

2 Dewsbury 2012.

3 Edwards et al. 2012.

4 Ibid.

5 Pew Research Center 2015, 18. The findings in this survey draw on data from two primary sources: a nationally representative survey of 1,555 multiracial Americans ages 18 and older, conducted online from February 6 to April 6, 2015, and Pew Research analyses of data collected by the US Census Bureau. In the Pew study, White/Native American people constituted the largest multiracial group in the study (half), while Black/Native American people comprised 12 percent, Black/White people 11 percent, and Asian/White people 4 percent.

6 See Aspinall and Song 2013.

7 McDonald 2013.

8 *Guardian Online* 2015.

9 Ibid.

10 Kirton 2016.

11 Douglas 1966.

12 Tyler 2008.

13 See the critiques by Morning 2014; Skinner 2011; Nelson 2008; Byrd and Hughey 2015.

14 Song 2003.

15 See Brubaker 2016 for an excellent discussion of this controversy.

16 Parker and Song 2001, Introduction.

17 While "Mixed" was used in the 2001 England and Wales census, the 2011 census used the category "Mixed/multiple ethnic groups" to convey the possibility of more than two ancestries. I use the shorthand "mixed" throughout.

18 Aspinall and Song 2013.

19 Berthoud 1998.

20 Office for National Statistics 2005.

21 It's clear that the 2005 ONS does not mean people who are of disparate *ethnic* parentages (such as French and English, or Black Jamaican and Black Nigerian); rather, it is concerned with people of disparate *racial* ancestries. See Song 2015.

22 In an analysis of the 2011 England and Wales Census, "inter-ethnic unions" are said to be any unions in which partners identify themselves differently—that is, partners who choose different "tick boxes" among the 18 possible categories are categorized as constituting an "inter-ethnic" union (Office for National Statistics 2014). Thus, partners who may have identified themselves as "White and Black African" and "White and Black Caribbean," respectively, were counted as "inter-ethnic" (despite a shared Black heritage), just as partners who identified as "Irish" and "Caribbean," respectively, were.

23 Nelson 2008.

24 Giddens 1991.

25 For instance, see Joshua Gamson's (2015) illuminating study of "modern families," including homosexual couples and their families.

26 Office for National Statistics 2012.

27 Davenport 2016.

28 Bryman 2004; Creswell 1998.

29 Silverman 2013.

30 Strauss and Corbin 1990, 61.

CHAPTER 1. MULTIRACIAL PEOPLE AS PARENTS

1 Parker and Song 2001, 1.

2 Ifekwunigwe 2004.

3 See the classic works of Park 1928 and Stonequist 1937.

4 Song 2003, chap. 4.

5 Ali 2003; Caballero 2012; Benson 1983.

6 See, for example, Anzaldua 1987 on a border-crossing "mestiza consciousness" and Spickard 2001 on the boom in multiracial autobiographies.

7 Root 1992; Root 1996c.

8 Starting with *Mixed blood*, in 1989, Paul Spickard has been a prolific scholar of multiracial people and their lives across various societies.

9 For instance, see Kich 1992.

10 Root 1996a, xxi–xxii.

11 Root 1996b.

12 Parker and Song 2001 emphasize this point in their introduction; see also the work of Rosalind Edwards and Chamion Caballero.

13 Caballero 2012; Song and Gutierrez 2016.

14 Pew Survey 2015, 15.

15 See Saenz et al. 1995; Xie and Goyette 1997; Brunsma 2005; Qian 2004.

16 A number of variables, such as neighborhood diversity, the sex of the minority parent, and educational backgrounds, have been considered in such analyses. For

instance, in the case of households with mixed Asian/White children, higher educational attainment is associated with a greater likelihood that the child will be classified as Asian (Saenz et al. 1995). By comparison, Xie and Goyette (1997) found that having a parent who speaks an Asian language, an Asian father, and a residence in a location with many other Asians, all influence the likelihood that a child would be identified solely as Asian.

17 Davenport 2016; Roth 2005; Rockequemore and Brunsma 2002; Bratter 2007; DaCosta 2007; Nobles 2000.

18 See Lee and Bean 2010.

19 Roth 2005.

20 Other scholars have also argued that a higher socioeconomic background for multiracial people, including Black/White individuals, may predispose them to report themselves and their children in a variety of ways (see Korgen 2010; Faghen-Smith 2010; but see also Bratter 2010).

21 Liebler 2016.

22 Rockequemore, Brunsma, and Delgado 2009.

23 Holloway, Wright, and Ellis 2012, 76.

24 Brunsma 2005.

25 Gallagher 2004.

26 Rockequemore and Arend 2002, 61.

27 Saperstein and Penner 2012; and see Davenport 2016.

28 Brunsma 2005, 1151.

29 Caballero, Edwards, and Puthussery 2008; Spickard 1989; Zack 1996; Aspinall and Song 2013.

30 For example, see Twine 2010 and Tizard and Phoenix 1993. However, a book by Sharon Chang (2016) about parents of multiracial Asian children in the United States has recently appeared. See also Standen 1996.

31 Barn 1999; Mackenzie 2012; Harman 2010; Twine 2010; Okitikpi 2005.

32 Roth 2005, 41.

33 Rockequemore and Laszloffy 2005.

34 Rockequemore and Brunsma 2002; Khanna 2011; Campbell and Troyer 2007; Roth 2012; DaCosta 2007; Root 1996c.

35 Campbell and Eggerling-Boeck 2006.

36 See for instance Barn 2013; Peters 2016; Kirton 2000; Barn and Kirton 2012; Vonk and Massatti 2008.

37 See Kanaiapuni and Liebler 2005 for one of the few US studies on this topic. There is also the work of social psychologists such as Diane Hughes.

38 Caballero, Edwards, and Puthussery 2008. See also Caballero, Edwards, and Smith 2008.

39 Aspinall and Song 2013.

40 Holloway, Wright, and Ellis 2012, 88.

41 Office for National Statistics 2012.

42 In fact, as Lucinda Platt (2012) has pointed out, current quantitative analysis of mixed people in Britain is still mostly descriptive, and thus much of the framing and analysis of determinants regarding the multiracial population has been in relation to studies in the United States.

43 Nandi and Platt 2012.

44 For Britain, see Berthoud 1998; for the United States, see Gullickson and Morning 2011.

45 Aspinall 2009; Morning 2008; Roth 2012; Simon, Piché, and Gagnon 2015.

46 Aspinall 2015.

47 Aspinall and Song 2013.

48 Bradford 2006; Coleman 2010.

49 Coleman 2010.

50 Patten 2015.

51 Benson 1983; Wilson 1987.

52 See Song 2010a; Ali 2003; Bauer 2010; Edwards and Caballero 2008; Alibhai-Brown 2001; Ifekwunigwe 1999; Tizard and Phoenix 1993; Olumide 2002.

53 Caballero, Edwards, and Puthussery 2008; Ali 2003; Twine 2010; Barn 1999; Harman 2010; Okitikpi 2005; Tizard and Phoenix 1993; Katz 1996.

54 Aspinall and Song 2013.

55 Panico and Nazroo 2011; and see Caballero, Edwards, and Smith 2008.

56 Song 2010b; Platt 2012.

57 Peters 2016.

58 *Economist* 2014.

59 Ibid; and see Muttarak and Heath 2010.

60 See the volume edited by King-O'Riain et al. 2014.

61 Morning 2008.

62 See the volume edited by Simon, Piché, and Gagnon 2015.

63 See Twine 1997; Daniel 2006; Telles 2004.

64 See Sue 2014.

65 See the volume edited by Spickard 2013.

66 See Mahtani 2002; Mahtani, Kwan-Lafond, and Taylor 2014.

67 See Luke and Luke 1998; Fozdar and Perkins 2014.

68 See Welty 2014; Lie 2004.

69 Platt 2009.

70 Tashiro 2002; Khanna 2004.

71 Parker and Song 2001.

72 Brubaker 1992; Wimmer 2013.

73 Brubaker 1992.

74 Office for National Statistics 2005.

75 Ibid.

76 See Twine and Gallagher 2008; Lee and Bean 2004.

77 Rondilla and Spickard 2007; Herring, Keith, and Horton 2004; Rockquemore and Arend 2002.

78 Song and Gutierrez 2015.

79 Ibid.

80 Ali 2003. And see Gilroy 1998.

81 Hylton et al. 2011.

82 Silverman and Yuval-Davis 1999.

83 See Banton 1998.

84 Mahtani and Moreno 2001; and see Gambol 2016 for an interesting study of second generation Filipino Americans' unions with other Asian Americans and other non-White individuals such as Latinos and Blacks.

85 Kanaiapuni and Liebler 2005.

86 Herman 2011; Morning 2000.

87 This point is made by Davenport (2016, 59).

88 Pew survey 2015, 13.

89 Shih et al. 2007.

90 See Bratter 2007.

91 Rockquemore and Laszloffy 2005. As McKibbin (2014, 195) points out, "Children [in interracial households] are generally socialized by monoracial parents with clear links to monoracial groups."

92 Phillips, Odunlami, and Bonham 2007; Waters 1990.

93 According to Craemer (2010, 308): "Since we inherit only one random half of our DNA from each parent and lose the other random half, the chance of identifying actual biological ancestors through genetic matching decreases by 50% with each generation we go back in time. At the same time, however, the actual number of ancestors doubles. Thus, any two individuals are increasingly likely to share a common ancestor, and increasingly unlikely to know about that shared ancestor, with every generation we go back in their family trees."

94 Aspinall and Song 2013; and see Morning 2000.

CHAPTER 2. HOW DO MULTIRACIAL PEOPLE IDENTIFY THEIR CHILDREN?

1 Pew Survey 2015. Craemer (2010) also argues that knowledge about ancestors of other backgrounds (what he calls "ancestral ambivalence") may predict response instability in racial self-classification.

2 Skinner 2011, 116.

3 David Brunsma (2006b) has observed that how one classifies oneself publicly may differ from how one may identify in various personal scenarios.

4 Brubaker 2015; Roth 2016.

5 Bratter 2007, 822. Using the 5 percent Public Use Microdata Sample of the 2000 US Census, Bratter, examines four types of multiracial families in which the parents (all non-Hispanic) are: White/non-White, Black/non-Black, Asian/non-Asian, and American Indian/non-American Indian. See also Bratter 2010, in which the analysis focuses specifically on households in which one parent is

(single race) Black and the other parent is not, as well as a further examination of cases where one parent is *partially* Black.

6 Bratter 2010, 189.

7 Bratter 2007, 841.

8 Bratter 2010, 190. In the case of the 2000 US census (in which people could nominate multiple racial categories), census reports reveal that 53 percent of children identified with more than one race in the US were in households where at least one parent was identified with multiple races (Tafoya, Johnson, and Hill 2004). This is not surprising, since one would expect, at least in many cases, a correspondence between a parent's racial identity (as multiracial) and the way in which she may racially identify her children (as multiracial). This also suggests that first-generation mixed parents can engage in the inter-generational transmission of multiple ancestries to their second-generation children.

9 Bratter (2010, 193) found that in the case of "children of a Black-White mother and a White father (i.e., where the 'White' racial background is shared) over half [59 percent] are labeled as multiracial but less than 40 percent [39.8 percent] are labeled as 'White.'" But it is striking that as many as 39.8 percent of such interracial couplings actually classified their children as *White*. Very similar results were also found for a *Black/White father* and a White mother, though in such households with a Black/White father, just under 33 percent classified their children as White and almost 65 percent classified their children as multiracial—suggesting a gendered dimension to this process.

10 Rockquemore, Laszloffy, and Noveske 2006.

11 Bratter and Heard 2009, 661.

12 Song 2003, chap. 4.

13 As was found with *some* multiracial parents who had minority partners (with whom they shared a racial overlap) in the United States (Bratter 2007).

14 Bratter 2007; 2010.

15 Song and Gutierrez 2015.

16 In the United States, Jenifer Bratter's (2010, 201) study of how partially Black and single-race Black parents identified their children also found "a good deal of intersection between 'Black' and 'multiracial' within households."

17 Song and Hashem 2010.

18 Dyer 1997; Frankenberg 1993.

19 See Tashiro 2002; Song and Hashem 2010.

20 And see Harris and Sim 2002.

21 Song and Hashem 2010.

22 Bratter 2010; 2007.

CHAPTER 3. THE PARENTING PRACTICES OF MULTIRACIAL PEOPLE

1 Kich 1992; Rockquemore and Laszloffy 2005.

2 Rockquemore and Laszloffy 2005, 59.

3 Rockquemore, Laszloffy, Noveske 2006.
4 Caballero, Edwards, Puthussery 2008.
5 Pew survey 2015, 60.
6 Barn 2013, 1275.
7 Bratter 2007, 825.
8 See Twine 2010 and Harman 2010.
9 Twine 2010.
10 Rockquemore, Laszloffy, and Noveske 2006; Barn 2013.
11 Caballero et al. 2012.
12 Bratter and Heard 2009.
13 Morgan 1996, 24.
14 See Davenport 2016; Khanna 2011; Waters 1999, for studies in the USA. In Britain, Aspinall and Song 2013 also found that mixed race women of various mixed backgrounds were more likely to report that their mixed backgrounds were viewed positively by others than the mixed men in their study.
15 See Gans 1979; Waters 1990; for excellent discussions of optional ethnicities in the USA.
16 For a fascinating foray into understandings of (and negotiations around) ethnic authenticity, see Ang 2001; also Song 2003. Many of the East Asian/White participants in this study expressed ongoing feelings of self-consciousness around other "full" Asian people.
17 King-O'Riain 2006; and see Mengel's 2001 discussion of a harrowing interaction in Japantown, San Francisco.
18 Song and Gutierrrez 2015.
19 Though not about multiracial people, per se, Karyn Lacy (2004) found that middle class African Americans who worked or lived in predominantly White spaces demonstrated a form of "strategic assimilation" into such White spaces, but made efforts to "consciously retain their connections to the black world as well." (910)
20 Appiah 2006; Anderson 2011; Gilroy 2004.
21 Vertovec 2007.
22 See the findings of Caballero, Edwards, and Puthussery 2008.
23 Faghen-Smith 2010; see also Davenport 2016. But in the case of Black and partially Black couples in the United States, Bratter (2010, 200) found that the racial classification of their children was "insensitive" to levels of education or family income.
24 Anderson 2011.
25 See Caballero, Edwards, and Smith 2008; also Caballero, Edwards, and Puthussery 2008.
26 Caballero et al. 2012.

CHAPTER 4. MULTIRACIAL PEOPLE, THEIR CHILDREN, AND RACISM
1 Jenkins 1996; Aspinall and Song 2013.
2 Goldberg 1990.

3 In Song (2014), I argue against what I call a "culture of racial equivalence," which has become rife in Britain.

4 See Wellman 1977; Feagin 2000; Desmond and Emirbayer 2009; Desmond and Emirbayer 2016. And for their influential discussion of "racial formation" in the USA, see Omi and Winant (1994).

5 See especially the work of Eduardo Bonilla-Silva (2001; 2003); in Britain, similar arguments have been made by Barker (1981) and Rattansi (2007), among others.

6 Bonilla-Silva 2003.

7 Office for National Statistics 2005; Ford 2008.

8 See Herring, Keith, and Horton 2004; Hunter 2007; Hochschild and Weaver 2007.

9 Campbell and Herman 2010.

10 Herman 2004.

11 Khanna 2011.

12 Sharon Chang's (2016) book about raising multiracial Asian children in the United States counters the suggestion made by some prominent US social scientists that many multiracial Asians are effectively honorary Whites who do not encounter negative racial stereotypes or interactions.

13 Pew Survey 2015, 8.

14 Aspinall and Song 2013; Tizard and Phoenix 1993; Brunsma and Rockquemore 2001; Herman 2004; Tashiro 2002.

15 Smith and Moore 2000; Mengel 2001.

16 Song 2014.

17 Cheng and Lee 2009, 53.

18 See Spickard 1989; Mengel 2001.

19 Song 2010.

20 Feagin 2000; Bonilla-Silva 2003.

21 Barker 1981.

22 Back 1996, 53.

23 Song 2014; Back 1996.

24 Bonilla-Silva 2003.

25 Rockquemore and Laszloffy 2005,59.

26 Song 2003, chaps. 3 and 4.

27 In fact, some research suggests that Black families engage more actively in discussions of prejudice than families from White or other ethnic minority backgrounds (Hughes et al. 2006).

28 Lee et al. 2012; Solomos and Back 1996; Gilroy 2000.

29 While one must be cautious about cultural generalizations, social psychologists have noted the role that cultural norms and gender can play in how disparate ethnic groups, such as Asian Americans and African Americans, respond differently to instances of racism (see, for example, Lee et al. 2012).

30 See, among others, Rockquemore and Laszloffy 2005; Twine and Gallagher 2008.

31 See Chang (2016) for discussion of the racisms encountered by multiracial Americans with Asian ancestries. See also Song and Hashem (2010).

32 See Barber 2015.

33 Kim 1999.

34 Foner 2015. And see Alba and Foner (2015), for an exploration of immigrant integration in Europe (France, Germany, Great Britain, the Netherlands), the United States and Canada, and how this process is fundamentally shaped by both religion and race, among other variables.

35 Alexander 2000; Modood et al. 1997; McGhee 2005.

36 Younge 2010; Modood 1996; Lewis 2007.

37 Muttarak and Heath 2010.

38 Back 1996; Alexander 2000.

CHAPTER 5. THE FUTURE

1 Because the interview took place in Josh's home, the interviewer felt unable to dissuade Alicia from joining in the discussion; both Josh and she seemed to want to discuss these issues together.

2 Childs 2006, 236.

3 Caballero 2012. Various television programs have also explored this theme in Britain, such as Channel 4's provocatively titled program, "Is it better to be mixed race?" (aired November 2, 2009), in which a geneticist (and mother of mixed children) poses the question of whether mixed people possess a biological advantage in their "make-up."

4 Brubaker 1992; Wimmer 2013.

5 Pew Survey 2015, 9.

6 In addition to the defacing of mosques and anti-Muslim graffiti in various parts of the country, there have also been hostility and various hate crimes directed at Polish migrants. For instance, post-Brexit, some people of Polish heritage have been told to speak English if they were heard speaking Polish in public places. Polish men have also been attacked in parts of Britain. www.theguardian.com.

7 Rushdie 1991, 394.

8 Hall 1992, 310.

9 Hall 1992.

CONCLUSION

1 In relation to the United States, Bratter (2007, 827) noted that "if multiracial parents classify their children as single-race individuals, racial distinctions and thus racial boundaries may remain intact even as interracial interaction increases." In the case of the multiracial participants in this study, such a scenario seems unlikely in the British context, given the number of people (of all mixed types) who insisted that their children, too, were mixed.

2 See the earlier discussion of Bratter (2007; 2010) in chapter 2.

3 Roth 2005; Bratter 2007.

4 However, the second generation children of first-generation Black/White participants were more likely to be racially assigned to their minority race than were the other mixed participants.

5 Michael Banton (1997) has argued that people's ethnic and racial consciousness and their use of ethnic and racial categories (wholly socially constructed) vary according to their specific circumstances and are undergirded by their interests and the social structures surrounding them.

6 Feliciano 2016.

7 While there is no one perspective on this question, the edited volumes by Root (1992; 1996) suggest potential commonalities among various types of multiracial people. See also Mahtani and Moreno (2001); Mengel (2001).

8 The killing of many Black men, such as Trayvon Martin in 2012, and the emergence of the Black Lives Matter movement in the United States, has certainly been influential in forging a trans-Atlantic understanding of Blackness and Black experiences more generally. Unlike in the United States, however, in Britain contested understandings of who is "Black" still arise. Many official documents (and institutions such as universities) and media outlets use the acronym BME (Black and minority ethnic) to refer to non-White minority people, but this usage is regarded by many as problematic, as this term is seen to lump together non-White Britons with very different racial histories and experiences. In late October 2016, the student union at the University of Kent was much criticized (dubbed a "national embarrassment" by many Kent students) for using the image of the One Direction star Zayn Malik for their Black History Month poster—as he has no (known) African ancestry (see Batty 2016). Rather, Malik's image was meant to convey a broader, political understanding of Blackness (see Modood 1994 for a discussion of the term "Black" in the British context).

9 For instance, see Lee and Bean 2010; Yancey 2006.

10 Ogbu 1990.

11 Liebler 2016.

12 Aspinall and Song 2013; and see the rates of "interethnic" unions in the Office for National Statistics (2012).

13 This finding resonates with that of Tashiro (2002, 16): the mixed African American participants she interviewed "have an affinity for blackness that was not consistently expressed by the mixed Asian American group for their Asian heritages. According to what the mixed African Americans told me, that affinity is made up of a complex mix of loyalty, safety, comfort, shared history, lack of choice, and the common experience of the pain of racism." However, those mixed Asian Americans who had reported experiencing racism reported similar levels of a group identity as multiracial.

14 See Parker 1995; Song 1999; Barber 2015.

15 Younge 2010.

16 See the studies of Twine 2010; Tyler 2005.

17 Bonilla-Silva 2003; Rockquemore, Laszloffy, and Noveske 2006; Childs 2006; among many others. See Chapter 4 of this book for a fuller discussion of racism.

18 But see Tashiro 2011; Chang 2016; Rondilla and Spickard 2007; Khanna 2004, Mahtani, and Moreno 2001; See Chapter 1 of this book for a fuller review of the extant literature.

19 Gilroy (2000, 12–13) writes that "the demise of 'race' is not something to be feared," but a necessary step in opposing and ultimately destroying racial hierarchies and ideologies.

20 Saperstein and Penner 2012, 676. As the authors observe, "By exploring whether race changes over time [in terms of both racial self-identification and how others classify someone], partly in response to changes in an individual's social position, we shift from treating race as a fixed characteristic of individuals to thinking about it as a propensity to identify or be classified in a particular way at a particular point in time." Davenport (2016) also argues that, generally speaking, a more privileged class position is associated with the tendency to "whiten" one's racial identification.

21 Ford 2015.

22 Spickard 2003.

23 Craemer 2010.

24 Parker and Song 2001, Introduction.

25 Spickard 2015. And see Hollinger 1995.

26 Jimenez 2010.

27 Ibid.

28 Brubaker 2015, 3.

29 Nelson 2016. Also see Roth and Lyon 2016.

30 See for instance the now classic studies by Gordon (1964) and Portes and Zhou (1993). See also Alba and Nee 2003.

31 Nagel 1995.

32 Song 2009.

33 See Waters 1990; Phillips, Odunlami, and Bonham 2007.

34 Pew Survey 2015, 42.

35 Song 2010a.

36 Song 2015.

37 But see Gullickson and Morning 2011; Liebler 2016; Song 2015.

38 McKibbin 2014, 185.

39 Aspinall 2015; Aspinall and Song 2013.

40 Song 2015.

41 Kim 1999; Song 2014.

42 Fhagen-Smith 2010.

REFERENCES

Alba, Richard, and Nancy Foner. 2015. *Strangers no more*. Princeton, NJ: Princeton University Press.

Alba, Richard, and Victor Nee. 2003. *Remaking of mainstream America*. Cambridge, MA: Harvard University Press.

Alexander, Claire. 2000. *The Asian gang*. Oxford: Berg.

Ali, Suki. 2003. *Mixed-race, post-race*. Oxford: Berg.

Alibhai-Brown, Yasmin. 2001. *Mixed feelings: The complex lives of mixed race Britons*. London: Women's Press.

Ang, Ien. 2001. *On not speaking Chinese*. London: Routledge.

Anderson, Elijah. 2011. *The cosmopolitan canopy*. New York: W. W. Norton.

Anzaldua, Gloria. 1987. *Borderlands: The new mestiza*. San Francisco: Spinsters/Aunt Lute.

Appiah, Anthony. 2006. *Cosmopolitanism*. New York: W. W. Norton.

Aspinall, Peter. 2009. The future of ethnicity classifications. *Journal of Ethnic and Migration Studies* 35(9):1417–35.

———. 2015. Social representations of "mixed-race" in early twenty-first-century Britain, *Ethnic and Racial Studies* 38:1067–83.

Aspinall, Peter, and Miri Song. 2013. *Mixed race identities*. Basingstoke: Palgrave Macmillan.

Asthana, Anushka, and David Smith. 2009. Revealed: The rise of mixed-race Britain, *Observer*, January 18. www.theguardian.com.

Back, Les. 1996. *New ethnicities*. London: University College London Press.

Banton, Michael. 1997. *Ethnic and racial consciousness*, 2nd edition. Harlow: Addison Wesley Longman.

———. 1998. *Racial theories*. Cambridge: Cambridge University Press.

Barber, Tamsin. 2015. *Oriental identities in super-diverse Britain*. London: Palgrave Macmillan.

Barker, Martin. 1981. *The new racism*. London: Junction Books.

Barn, Ravinder. 1999. White mothers, mixed parentage children and child welfare. *British Journal of Social Work* 29(2):269–84.

———. 2013. "Doing the right thing": Transracial adoption in the USA. *Ethnic and Racial Studies* 36(8):1273–91.

Barn, Ravinder, and Derek Kirton. 2012. Transracial adoption in Britain: Politics, ideology and reality. *Adoption and Fostering* 36(3):25–37.

Batty, David. 2016. Student union promotes Black history month with Zayn Malik picture. Guardian.com, October 26. www.theguardian.com.

Bauer, Elaine. 2010. *The Creolisation of London kinship*, Amsterdam: Amsterdam University Press.

Benson, Susan. 1983. *Ambiguous ethnicity*. Cambridge: Cambridge University Press.

Berthoud, Richard. 1998. Defining ethnic groups: Origin or identity? *Patterns of Prejudice* 32:53–63.

Blow, Charles. 2015. "The Delusions of Dolezal." *New York Times*, June 18. www.nytimes.com.

Bonilla-Silva, Eduardo. 2001. *White supremacy and racism in the post-civil rights era*. Boulder, CO: Lynne Rienner.

———. 2003. *Racism without racists*. New York: Rowman & Littlefield.

Bradford, Ben. 2006. Who is mixed? London: Office for National Statistics.

Bratter, Jenifer. 2007. Will "multiracial" survive to the next generation? *Social Forces* 86(2):821–49.

———. 2010. The "one drop rule" through a multiracial lens. In *Multiracial Americans and social class*, edited by K. Korgen, 184–204. Abingdon: Routledge.

Bratter, Jennifer, and Holly Heard. 2009. Mother's, father's, both: Parental gender and racial classification of multiracial adolescents. *Sociological Forum* 24(3):658–88.

Brubaker, Rogers. 1992. *Ethnicity without groups*. Cambridge, MA: Harvard University Press.

———. 2016. The Dolezal affair: Race, gender, and the micropolitics of identity. *Ethnic and Racial Studies* 39(3):414–48.

Brunsma, David. 2005. Interracial families and the racial identification of mixed-race children: Evidence from the early childhood longitudinal study. *Social Forces* (84)2:1131–57.

Brunsma, David, ed. 2006a. *Mixed messages: Multiracial identities in the "color-blind" era*. Boulder, CO: Lynne Rienner.

Brunsma, David. 2006b. Public categories, private identities. *Social Science Research* 35:555–76.

Brunsma, David, and Kerry Ann Rockquemore. 2001. The new color complex: Appearances and biracial identity. *Identity* 1(3):225–246.

Bryman, Alan. 2004. *Social research methods*. Oxford: Oxford University Press.

Byrd, Carson, and Matthew Hughey. 2015. Biological determinism and racial essentialism. *Annals of the American Academy of Political and Social Sciences* 661:8–22.

Caballero, Chamion. 2012. From "Draughtboard Alley" to "Brown Britain": The ordinariness of racial mixing and mixedness in British society. In *International perspectives on racial mixing and mixedness*, edited by R. Edwards, S. Ali, C. Caballero, and M. Song, 36–56. London: Routledge.

Caballero, Chamion, R. Edwards, A. Goodyer, and T. Okitikpi. 2012. The diversity and complexity of the everyday lives of mixed racial and ethnic families. *Adoption and Fostering* 36:9–24.

Caballero, Chamion, Ros Edwards, and Shubi Puthussery. 2008. Parenting "mixed" children: Difference and belonging in mixed race and faith families. London: Joseph Rowntree Foundation.

Caballero, Chamion, Ros Edwards, and Darren Smith. 2008. Cultures of mixing: Understanding partnerships across ethnicity. *Twenty-First Century Society: Journal of the Academy of Social Sciences* 3:49–63.

Campbell, Mary, and Jennifer Eggerling-Boeck. 2006. What about the children? *Sociological Quarterly* 47:147–73.

Campbell, Mary, and Melissa Herman. 2010. Politics and policies: Attitudes toward multiracial Americans. *Ethnic and Racial Studies* 33(9):1511–36.

Campbell, Mary, and Lisa Troyer. 2007. The implications of racial misclassification by observers. *American Sociological Review* 72(5):750–65.

Cantle, Ted. 2001. Community cohesion: A report of the independent review team. London: Home Office.

Chang, Sharon. 2016. *Raising mixed race: Multiracial Asian children in a post-racial world.* New York: Routledge.

Cheng, Chi-Ying, and Fiona Lee. 2009. Multiracial identity integration: Perceptions of conflict and distance among multiracial individuals. *Journal of Social Issues* 65:51–68.

Childs, Erica C. 2006. *Navigating interracial borders.* New Brunswick, NJ: Rutgers University Press.

Coleman, David. 2010. Projections of the ethnic minority populations of the United Kingdom 2006–2056. *Population and Development Review* 36(3):441–86.

Craemer, Thomas. 2010. Ancestral ambivalence and racial self-classification change. *Social Science Research* 47(2):307–25.

Creswell, John. 1998. *Qualitative inquiry and research design.* Thousand Oaks, CA: Sage.

DaCosta, Kimberly. 2007. *Making multiracials.* Stanford, CA: Stanford University Press.

Daniel, Reg. 1996. Black and White identity in the new millennium: Unsevering the ties that bind. In *Multiracial people in America*, edited by M. Root. 121–39. Thousand Oaks, CA: Sage.

———. 2006. *Race and multiraciality in Brazil and the United States: Converging paths?* University Park: Pennsylvania State University Press.

Davenport, Lauren. 2016. The role of gender, class, and religion in biracial Americans' racial labeling decisions. *American Sociological Review* 81(1):57–84.

Desmond, Matthew, and Mustafa Emirbayer. 2009. *Racial domination, racial progress.* New York: McGraw-Hill.

———. 2015. *Race in America.* New York: Norton.

Dewsbury, Rick. 2012. The NHS did not deserve to be so disgracefully glorified in this bonanza of left-wing propaganda. *Mail Online*, July 28.

Douglas, Mary. 1966. *Purity and danger.* London: Routledge.

Dyer, Richard. 1997. *White.* London: Routledge.

Economist. 2014. Into the melting pot. February 8. www.economist.com.

Edwards, Rosalind, and Chamion Caballero. 2012. What's in a name? An exploration of the significance of personal naming of "mixed" children for parents from different racial, ethnic and faith backgrounds. *Sociological Review* 56(1):39–60.

Edwards, Rosalind, Suki Ali, Chamion Cabablero, and Miri Song, eds. 2012. *International perspectives on racial and ethnic mixedness and mixing.* London: Routledge.

Feagin, Joe. 2000. *Racist America.* New York: Routledge.

Feliciano, Cynthia. 2016. Shades of race: How phenotype and observer characteristics shape racial classification. *American Behavioral Scientist* 60(4):390–419.

Fhagen-Smith, Peony. 2010. Social class, racial/ethnic identity, and the psychology of "choice." In *Multiracial Americans and social class,* edited by K. Korgen, 30–38. London: Routledge.

Florio, Adrian. 2016. An emerging entry into America's multiracial vocabulary: "Blaxican." National Public Radio, March 8. www.npr.org.

Foner, Nancy. 2015. Is Islam in Western Europe like race in the United States? *Sociological Forum* 30(4):885–99.

Ford, Richard. 2008. Is racial discrimination in Britain declining? *British Journal of Sociology* 59(4):609–36.

Ford, VaNatta. 2015. Plasticity pushback: What happens to non-malleable Black bodies? Paper presented to Collegium for African American Research, Liverpool Hope University, June 25.

Fozdar, Farida, and Maureen Perkins. 2014. Antipodean mixed race: Australia and New Zealand. In *Global mixed race,* edited by Rebecca King-O'Riain, Stephen Small, Minelle Mahtani, Miri Song, and Paul Spickard, 119–43. New York: New York University Press, 119–43.

Frankenberg, Ruth. 1993. *White women, race matters.* Minneapolis: University of Minnesota Press.

Gallagher, Charles. 2004. Racial redistricting: Expanding the boundaries of Whiteness. In *The politics of multiracialism,* edited by H. Dalmage, 59–76. Albany: State University of New York Press.

Gambol, Brenda. 2016. Changing racial boundaries and mixed unions. *Ethnic and Racial Studies* 39(14):2621–40.

Gamson, Joshua. 2015. *Modern families.* New York: New York University Press.

Gans, Herbert. 1979. Symbolic ethnicity: The future of ethnic groups and cultures in America. *Ethnic and Racial Studies* 2(1):1–20.

Giddens, Anthony. 1991. *Modernity and self-identity: Self and society in the late modern age.* Stanford, CA: Stanford University Press.

Gilroy, Paul. 1998. Race ends here. *Ethnic and Racial Studies* 21(5):838–47.

——. 2000. *Between camps.* London: Penguin.

——. 2004. *After empire: Melancholia or convivial culture?* London: Routledge.

Goldberg, David Theo. 1990. *The anatomy of racism.* Minneapolis: University of Minnesota Press.

Gordon, Milton. 1964. *Assimilation in American life*. New York: Oxford University Press.

Guardian Online. 2015. Woman accidentally impregnated with Black man's sperm has legal case dismissed. September 5. www.theguardian.com.

Gullickson, Aaron, and Ann Morning. 2011. Choosing race: Multiracial ancestry and identification. *Social Science Research* 40(2):498–512.

Hall, Stuart. 1992. The question of cultural identity. In *Modernity and its futures*, edited by S. Hall, D. Held, and T. McGrew, 273–326. Cambridge: Polity Press (and Open University Press).

Harman, Vicki. 2010. Experiences of racism and the changing nature of white privilege among lone white mothers of mixed-parentage children. *Ethnic and Racial Studies* 33(2):176–94.

Harris, David, and Jeremiah Sim. 2002. Who is multiracial? Assessing the complexity of lived race. *American Sociological Review* 67:614–27.

Herman, Melissa. 2004. Forced to choose: Some determinants of racial identification in multiracial adolescents. *Child Development* 75(3):730–48.

——. 2011. Methodology and measurement in the study of multiracial Americans: Identity, classification, and perceptions. *Sociology Compass* 5(7):607–17.

Herring, Cedric, V. Keith, and H. Horton, eds. 2004. *Skin deep: How race and complexion matter in the "color blind" era*. Urbana: University of Illinois Press.

Hirsch, Afua. 2016. Prince Harry, Meghan Markle, and the myth of royal purity. *Guardian*, November 2. www.theguardian.com.

——. Forthcoming 2017. *Brit(ish)*. London: Jonathon Cape.

Hochschild, Jennifer, and Vesla Weaver. 2007. The skin color paradox and the American racial order. *Social Forces* 86(2):643–70.

Hollinger, David. 1995. *Postethnic America*. New York: Basic Books.

Holloway, Steven, Richard Wright, and Mark Ellis. 2012. Constructing multiraciality in US families and neighbourhoods. In *International perspectives on racial and ethnic mixedness and mixing*, edited by R. Edwards, S. Ali, C. Caballero, and M. Song, 73–91. London: Routledge.

Hughes, D., J. Rodriguez, E. Smith, D. Johnson, H. C. Stevenson, and P. Spicer. 2006. Parents' ethnic/racial socialization: A review of research and directions for future study. *Developmental Psychology* 42:747–70.

Hunter, Margaret. 2007. The persistent problem of colorism. *Sociology Compass* 1(1):237–54.

Hylton, Kevin, Andrew Pilkington, Paul Warmington, and Shirin Housee, eds. 2011. *Atlantic crossings: International dialogues on critical race theory*. Birmingham: The Higher Education Academy, C-SAP.

Ifekwunigwe, Jayne. 1999. *Scattered belongings: Cultural paradoxes of race, nation and gender*, London: Routledge.

Ifekwunigwe, Jayne, ed. 2004. *"Mixed race" studies: A reader*. London: Routledge.

Jenkins, Richard. 1996. *Social identity*. London: Routledge.

Jimenez, Tomas. 2010. Affiliative ethnic identity. *Ethnic and Racial Studies* 33(10):1756–75.

Kanaiapuni, Shawn, and Carolyn Liebler. 2005. Pondering Poi Dog: Place and racial identification of multiracial native Hawaiians. *Ethnic and Racial Studies* 28(4):687–721.

Katz, Ilan. 1996. *The construction of racial identity in children of mixed parentage.* London: Jessica Kingsley Publishers.

Khanna, Nikki. 2004. The role of reflected appraisals in racial identity: The case of multiracial Asians. *Social Psychology Quarterly* 67(2):115–31.

——. 2011. *Biracial in America,* Lanham, MD: Lexington Books.

Kich, George K. 1992. The developmental process of asserting a biracial, bicultural identity. In *Racially mixed people in America,* edited by Maria Root, 304–17. Thousand Oaks, CA: Sage.

Kim, Claire Jean. 1999. The racial triangulation of Asian Americans. *Politics & Society* 27(1):105–38.

King-O'Riain, Rebecca. 2006. *Pure beauty: Judging race in Japanese American beauty pageants.* Minneapolis: University of Minnesota Press.

King-O'Riain, Rebecca, Stephen Small, Minelle Mahtani, Miri Song, and Paul Spickard, eds. 2014. *Global mixed race,* New York: New York University Press.

Kirton, Derek. 2000. *Race, ethnicity, and adoption.* Milton Keynes: Open University Press.

——. 2016. Neo-liberal racism: Excision, ethnicity and the Children and Families Act 2014. *Critical Social Policy* 36(4):1–20.

Korgen, Kathleen, ed. 2010. *Multiracial Americans and social class.* London: Routledge.

Lacy, Karyn. 2004. Black spaces, black places. *Ethnic and Racial Studies* 27 (6):908–30.

Lee, Elizabeth, Jose Soto, Janet Swim, and Michael Bernstein. 2012. Bitter reproach or sweet revenge: Cultural differences in response to racism. *Personality and Social Psychology Bulletin* 38(7):920–32.

Lee, Jennifer, and Frank Bean. 2004. America's changing color lines: Immigration, race/ethnicity, and multiracial identification. *Annual Review of Sociology* 30:221–42.

——. 2010. *The diversity paradox.* New York: Russell Sage Foundation.

Lewis, Philip. 2007. *Young, British, and Muslim.* London: Continuum.

Lie, John. 2004. *Multiethnic Japan.* Cambridge, MA: Harvard University Press.

Liebler, Carolyn. 2016. On the boundaries of race. *Sociology of Race and Ethnicity* 2(4):548–68.

Luke, Carmen, and Allan Luke. 1998. Interracial families: Difference within difference. *Ethnic and Racial Studies* 21(4):728–54.

Mackenzie, Liza. 2012. Finding value on a council estate. In *International perspectives on racial and ethnic mixedness and mixing,* edited by R. Edwards, S. Ali, C. Caballero, and M. Song, 92–107. London: Routledge.

Mahtani, Minelle. 2002. What's in a name? Exploring the employment of "mixed race" as an ethno-racial identification. *Ethnicities* 2(4):469–90.

Mahtani, Minelle, Dani Kwan-Lafond, and Leanne Taylor. 2014. Exporting the mixed race nation: Mixed-race identities in the Canadian context. In *Global mixed race*, edited by Rebecca King-O'Riain, Stephen Small, Minelle Mahtani, Miri Song, and Paul Spickard, 238–62. New York: New York University Press.

Mahtani, Minelle, and April Moreno. 2001. Same difference: Towards a more unified discourse in 'mixed race' theory. In *Rethinking "mixed race,"* edited by D. Parker and M. Song, 65–75. London: Pluto Press.

McDonald, Henry. 2013. Irish police return blonde girl to Roma family. October 24. *Guardian Online*. www.theguardian.com.

McGhee, Derek. 2005. *Intolerant Britain*. Maidenhead: Open University Press.

McKibbin, Molly. 2014. The current state of multiracial discourse. *Journal of Critical Mixed Race Studies* 1(1):183–202.

Mengel, Laurie. 2001. Triples—The social evolution of a multiracial panethnicity. In *Rethinking "mixed race,"* edited by D. Parker and M. Song, 99–116. London: Pluto Press.

Modood, Tariq. 1994. Political Blackness and British Asians. *Sociology* 28(4):859–76.

———. 1996. The changing context of "race" in Britain. *Patterns of Prejudice* 30(1):3–13.

———. 2005. *Multicultural politics: Racism, ethnicity, and Muslims in Britain*. Minneapolis: University of Minnesota Press.

Modood, Tariq, R. Berthoud, J. Lakey, J. Nazroo, P. Smith, S. Virdee, and S. Beishon. 1997. *Ethnic minorities in Britain: Diversity and disadvantage*. London: Policy Studies Institute.

Morgan, David. 1996. *Family connections: An introduction to family studies*. Cambridge: Polity Press.

Morning, Ann. 2000. Who is multiracial? Definitions and decisions. *Sociological Imagination* 37(4):209–29.

———. 2008. Ethnic classification in global perspective. *Population Research and Policy Review* 27(2):239–72.

———. 2014. And you thought we had moved beyond all that: Biological race returns to the social sciences. *Ethnic and Racial Studies Review* 37(10):1676–85.

Muttarak, Raya, and Anthony Heath. 2010. Who intermarries in Britain: Explaining ethnic diversity in intermarriage patterns. *British Journal of Sociology* 61:275–305.

Nagel, Joanne. 1995. American Indian renewal. *American Sociological Review* 60(6):947–65.

Nandi, Alita, and Lucinda Platt. 2012. How diverse is the UK? In *Understanding society: Findings 2012*, edited by S. McFall, 12–13. Colchester: Institute for Social and Economic Research, University of Essex.

Nandi, Miriam, and Paul Spickard. 2014. The curious career of the one-drop rule: Multiraciality and membership in Germany today. In *Global mixed race*, edited by Rebecca King-O'Riain, Stephen Small, Minelle Mahtani, Miri Song, and Paul Spickard, 188–212. New York: New York University Press.

Nelson, Alondra. 2008. Bio science: Genetic genealogy testing and the pursuit of African ancestry. *Social Studies of Science* 38:809–33.

——. 2016. *The Social life of DNA*. Boston: Beacon Press.

Nobles, Melissa. 2000. *Shades of citizenship*. Stanford, CA: Stanford University Press.

Office for National Statistics. 2005. Focus on ethnicity and identity. London: ONS. www.ons.gov.uk.

——. 2012. Ethnicity and national identity in England and Wales 2011. London: ONS. www.ons.gov.uk.

——. 2014. What does the 2011 census tell us about inter-ethnic relationships? London: ONS. www.ons.gov.uk.

Ogbu, John. 1990. Minority status and literacy in comparative perspective. *Daedalus* 119:141–69.

Okitikpi, Toyin. 2005. Identity and identification: How mixed parentage children adapt to a binary world. In *Working with children of mixed parentage*, edited by T. Okitikpi, 76–92. Lyme Regis: Russell House.

Olumide, Jill. 2002. *Raiding the gene pool: The social construction of mixed race*. London: Pluto Press.

Omi, Michael, and Howard Winant. 1994. *Racial formation in the United States*. New York: Routledge.

Panico, Lydia, and James Nazroo. 2011. The social and economic circumstances of mixed ethnicity children in the UK. *Ethnic and Racial Studies* 34(9):1421–44.

Park, Robert. 1928. Human migration and the marginal man. *American Journal of Sociology* 33(6):881–93.

Parker, David, and Miri Song, eds. 2001. *Rethinking "mixed race."* London: Pluto Press.

Patten, Eileen. 2015. Who is multiracial? Depends on how you ask. Pew Research Center, November 6. www.pewsocialtrends.org.

Peters, Fiona. 2016. *Fostering mixed race children*. London: Palgrave Macmillan.

Pew Research Center. 2015. Multiracial in America: Proud, diverse and growing in numbers. Washington, DC, June 11.

Phillips, Elizabeth, A. Odunlami, and V. Bonham. 2007. Mixed race: Understanding difference in the genome era. *Social Forces* 86(2):795–820.

Platt, Lucinda. 2009. Ethnicity and family: Relationships within and between ethnic groups: An analysis using the Labour Force Survey. Colchester: Institute for Social and Economic Research, University of Essex.

——. 2012. A descriptive account of those self-identifying as of mixed ethnicity in Great Britain. In *International perspectives on racial and ethnic mixedness and mixing*, edited by R. Edwards, S. Ali, C. Caballero, and M. Song, 108–24. London: Routledge.

Portes, Alejandro, and Min Zhou. 1993. The new second generation: Segmented assimilation and its variants. *Annals of the American Academy of Political and Social Sciences* 530:74–96.

Qian, Zenchao. 2004. Options: Racial/ethnic identification of children of intermarried couples. *Social Science Quarterly* 85:746–66.

Rattansi, Ali. 2007. *Racism: A very short introduction*. Oxford: Oxford University Press.

Rockquemore, Kerry Ann, and Patricia Arend. 2002. Opting for White: Fluidity and racial identity construction in post–civil rights America. *Race & Society* 5:49–64.

Rockquemore, Kerry Ann, and David Brunsma. 2002. *Beyond Black: Biracial identity in America*. Thousand Oaks, CA: Sage.

Rockquemore, Kerry Ann, David Brunsma, and Daniel Delgado. 2009. Racing to theory or retheorizing race? *Journal of Social Issues* 65(1):13–34.

Rockquemore, Kerry Ann, and Tracey Laszloffy. 2005. *Raising biracial children*, Lanham, MD: Rowman.

Rockquemore, Kerry Ann, Tracey Laszloffy, and Julia Noveske. 2006. It all starts at home: Racial socialization in multiracial families. In *Mixed messages*, edited by D. Brunsma, 203–216. Boulder, CO: Lynne Rienner.

Rondilla, Joanne, and Paul Spickard. 2007. *Is lighter better?* Lanham, MD: Rowman & Littlefield.

Root, Maria, ed. 1992. *Racially mixed people in America*. Thousand Oaks, CA: Sage.

Root, Maria. 1996a. The multiracial experience: Racial borders as a significant frontier in race relations. In *The multiracial experience*, edited by M. Root ix–xiii. Thousand Oaks, CA: Sage.

——. 1996b. A bill of rights for racially mixed people. In *The multiracial experience*, edited by M. Root, 3–14. Thousand Oaks, CA: Sage.

Root, Maria, ed. 1996c. *The multiracial experience*. Thousand Oaks, CA: Sage.

Roth, Wendy. 2005. The end of the one-drop rule? Labeling of multiracial children in Black intermarriages. *Sociological Forum* 20:35–67.

——. 2012. *Race migrations*. Palo Alto, CA: Stanford University Press.

——. 2016. The multiple dimensions of race. *Ethnic and Racial Studies* 39(8):1310–38.

Roth, Wendy and Katherine Lyon. 2016. Genetic ancestry tests and race. In *Reconsidering race: Cross-disciplinary and interdisciplinary approaches*, edited by K. Suzuki and D. von Vacano. New York, Oxford University Press.

Rushdie, Salman. 1991. *Imaginary homelands*. London: Granta.

Saenz, Rogelio, Sean Hwang, Benigno Aguirre, and Robert Anderson. 1995. Persistence and change in Asian identity among children of intermarried couples. *Sociological Perspectives* 38(2):175–94.

Saperstein, Aliya, and Andrew Penner. 2012. Racial fluidity and inequality in the United States. *American Journal of Sociology* 118(3):676–727.

Shih, M., C. Bonam, D. Sanchez, and C. Peck. 2007. The social construction of race: biracial identity and vulnerability to stereotypes. *Cultural Diversity and Ethnic Minority Psychology* 13(2):125–33.

Silverman, David. 2013. *Doing qualitative research*. London: Sage.

Silverman, Max, and Nira Yuval-Davis. 1999. Jews, Arabs and the theorisation of racism in Britain and France. In *Thinking identities*, edited by A. Brah, M. Hickman, and M. Mac an Ghaill, 25–48. Basingstoke, Macmillan.

Simon, Patrick, Victor Piché, and Amélie Gagnon, eds. 2015. *Social statistics and ethnic diversity*. New York: Springer.

Skinner, David. 2011. How might critical race theory allow us to rethink racial categorisation? In *Atlantic crossings*, edited by K. Hylton, A. Pilkington, P. Warmington, and S. Housee, 115–31. London: Open University Press.

Smith, Sandra, and Mignon Moore. 2010. Intraracial diversity and relations among African-Americans. *American Journal of Sociology* 106(1):1–39.

Solomos, John, and Les Back. 1996. *Racism and society*. London: Routledge.

Song, Miri. 2003. *Choosing ethnic identity*. Cambridge: Polity Press.

——. 2009. Is intermarriage a good indicator of integration? *Journal of Ethnic and Migration Studies* 35(2):331–48.

——. 2010a. Does "race" matter? A study of mixed race siblings' identifications. *Sociological Review* 58(2):265–85..

——. 2010b. Is there "a" mixed race group in Britain? *Critical Social Policy* 30(3):337–58.

——. 2014. Challenging a culture of racial equivalence. *British Journal of Sociology* 65(1):107–29.

——. 2015. What constitutes intermarriage for multiracial people in Britain? *Annals of the American Academy of Political and Social Sciences* 662:94–111.

Song, Miri, and Caitlin O. Gutierrez. 2015. "Keeping the story alive": Is ethnic and racial dilution inevitable for multiracial people and their children? *Sociological Review* 63(3):680–98.

——. 2016. What are the parenting practices of multiracial people in Britain? *Ethnic and Racial Studies* 39(7):1128–49.

Song, Miri, and Ferhana Hashem. 2010. What does "White" mean? *Sociological Perspectives* 53(2):287–92.

Spencer, Rainier. 2006. New racial identities, old arguments: Continuing biological reification. In *Mixed messages*, edited by David Brunsma, 83–102. Boulder, CO: Lynne Rienner.

Spickard, Paul. 1989. *Mixed blood: Intermarriage and ethnic identity in twentieth-century America*. Madison: University of Wisconsin Press.

——. 2001. The boom in multiracial autobiography. In *Rethinking "mixed race,"* edited by D. Parker and M. Song, 76–98. London: Pluto Press.

——. 2003. Does multiraciality lighten? Me-too ethnicity and the whiteness trap. In *New faces in a changing America: Multiracial identity in 21st-century America*, edited by Loretta I. Winters and Herman L. DeBose, 289–300. Thousand Oaks, CA: Sage.

——. 2015. Not passing—shape shifting: Reflections on racial plasticity. Paper presented to Mixed Heritage Conference, University of California, Los Angeles, April 25.

Spickard, Paul, ed. 2013. *Multiple identities: Migrants, ethnicity, and membership*. Bloomington: Indian University Press.

Standen, Brian. 1996. Without a template: The biracial Korean/White experiences. In *The multiracial experience*, edited by M. Root, 245–59. Thousand Oaks, CA: Sage.

Stonequist, Everett. 1937. *The marginal man*. New York: Russell and Russell.

Strauss, Anselm, and Juliet Corbin. 1990. *Basics of qualitative research*. Thousand Oaks, CA: Sage.

Sue, Christina. 2014. Negotiating identity narratives among Mexico's cosmic race. In *Global mixed race*, edited by Rebecca King-O'Riain, Stephen Small, Minelle Mahtani, Miri Song, and Paul Spickard, 144–66. New York: New York University Press.

Tafoya, Sonya, Hans Johnson, and Laura Hill. 2004. *Who chooses to choose two?* New York: Russell Sage Foundation.

Tashiro, Cathy. 2002. Considering the significance of ancestry through the prism of mixed-race identity. *Advances in Nursing Science* 25(2):1–21.

———. 2011. *Standing on both feet: Voices of older mixed race Americans*. Boulder, CO: Paradigm.

Telles, Edward. 2004. *Race in another America: The significance of skin color in Brazil*. Princeton, NJ: Princeton University Press.

Tizard, Barbara, and Ann Phoenix. 1993. *Black, White or mixed race? Race and racism in the lives of young people of mixed parentage*. London: Routledge.

Twine, France Winddance. 1997. *Racism in a racial democracy*. New Brunswick, NJ: Rutgers University Press.

———. 2010. *A White side of Black Britain*. Durham, NC: Duke University Press.

Twine, France, and Charles Gallagher. 2008. Introduction: The future of Whiteness. *Ethnic and Racial Studies* 31(1):4–24.

Tyler, Katharine. 2005. Genealogical imagination: The inheritance of interracial identities. *Sociological Review* 53(3):476–94.

———. 2008. Ethnographic approaches to race, genetics and genealogy. *Sociology Compass* 2(6):1860–77.

Vertovec, Steven. 2007. Super-diversity and its implications. *Ethnic and Racial Studies* 30(6):1024–54.

Vonk, Elizabeth, and Richard Massatti. 2008. Factors related to transracial adoptive parents' levels of cultural competence. *Adoption Quarterly* 11(3):204–26.

Waters, Mary. 1990. *Ethnic options: Choosing identity in America*. Berkeley: University of California Press.

———. 1999. *Black identities: West Indian immigrant dreams and American realities*. Cambridge, MA: Harvard University Press.

Wellman, David. 1977. *Portraits of White racism*. New York: Cambridge University Press.

Welty, Lily. 2014. Multiraciality and migration: Mixed-race American Okinawans, 1945–1972. In *Global mixed race*, edited by Rebecca King-O'Riain, Stephen Small, Minelle Mahtani, Miri Song, and Paul Spickard, 167–87. New York: New York University Press.

Wilson, Ann. 1987. *Mixed race children*. London: Unwin & Hyman.

Wimmer, Andreas. 2013. *Ethnic boundary making*. New York: Oxford University Press.

Xie, Yu, and Kimberley Goyette. 1997. The racial identification of biracial children with one Asian parent: Evidence from the 1990 census. *Social Forces* 76:547–70.

Yancey, George. 2006. Racial justice in a Black/Nonblack society. In *Mixed messages*, edited by David Brunsma, 49–62. Boulder, CO: Lynne Rienner.

Younge, Gary. 2010. *Who are we?* London: Penguin.

Zack, Naomi. 1996. On being and not-being Black and Jewish. In *Multiracial people in America*, edited by M. Root, 140–51. Thousand Oaks, CA: Sage.

INDEX

Black people and history:
  and importance of preserving the
    "Black line," 129–130, 133
  meaning of Black in Britain, 7, 79–80
  and objectification of Black people,
    132
  and racial consciousness of slavery and
    social injustice, 8, 30, 90, 117, 134,
    141–142, 154–156, 162
  role models, 117
  specificity of Black experience, 2, 8, 90,
    117, 119–121, 154–157
Black/White multiracial people:
  and cultivating appreciation of Black
    history and culture, 77–80, 156
  and discomfort with children partner-
    ing with White people, 129–134, 149
  "double mix" Black/White people,
    50–51
  and sense of commonality with other
    part Black or Black people, 49–51,
    155–156
  and those who identified primarily as
    White, 43–44, 54–55, 73–74, 157
Bratter, Jenifer, 37–39, 44, 62, 155
"Brexit" referendum, 147–148
Britishness (also Englishness):
  and its changing meanings with grow-
    ing diversity, 122, 145–147
  meanings of, 56–58, 60–61, 70–71
  and parents' negative views of English
    women as potential partners for
    their children, 129
  and physical appearance, 98–99

Brubaker, Rogers, 31, 159
Brunsma, David, 22–23

Caballero, Chamion, 3, 25, 66
Class:
  and assertion of mixed identities, 91
  and backgrounds of multiracial people,
    3, 24–25, 29
  middle-class multiracial people, 13, 91,
    106, 165
  and significance of, for racial identifi-
    cation, 13
  working-class multiracial people, 13,
    50, 81, 91, 121
Census (in UK and US):
  and categorization of multiracial
    people in US Census, 21–24, 33, 35,
    151
  and ethnicity question in Britain, 6,
    25–28
  and limitations of census "tick boxes"
    in studies, 8–10, 22–23, 33, 35, 37, 59,
    63, 151–152, 163
  who fills in the census form, 23, 37
  (see also Identification of children by
    multiracial parents)
Cosmopolitanism:
  as inclusivity, and acceptance of "differ-
    ent" people, 111–112, 144–147
  as main mode of parental socialization,
    82–88, 152
  as multiculture, 3, 144–147, 149
  and post-racial society, 84, 144–145,
    152, 155

ABOUT THE AUTHOR

Miri Song is Professor of Sociology at the University of Kent, England. She is the author of several books, including *Helping Out: Children's Labor in Ethnic Businesses*, *Choosing Ethnic Identity*, and (with Peter Aspinall) *Mixed Race Identities*. She is also the co-editor of three books on mixed-race people and their experiences.

Printed and bound by CPI Group (UK) Ltd, Croydon, CR0 4YY

09/06/2025

14685797-0001